INCULTURATION

Working Papers on Living Faith and Cultures

edited by

Arij A. Roest Crollius, S.J.

XII

CENTRE "CULTURES AND RELIGIONS" - PONTIFICAL GREGORIAN UNIVERSITY

STUART C. BATE, O.M.I.

EVANGELISATION
IN THE SOUTH AFRICAN CONTEXT

ROME 1991

Editrice Pontificia Università Gregoriana
Piazza della Pilotta, 35 - 00187 Roma

I N D E X

PRESENTATION

"Evangelisation" and "Context" appear to be the two living realities that support the process of inculturation. In the study of Fr. Stuart C. BATE, OMI, the context is that of South Africa. The ethnic, cultural and political diversity and tensions of this part of the African continent make of this particular context a macroscopic paradigm for Church-contexts in other parts of the world. This was one of the reasons that recommended the publication of this study in the series INCULTURATION.

The second reason is given by the fact that the South African context, precisely in its relevance for inculturation, has little been studied. The research done by the author of this work can serve as a practical introduction to the existant bibliography. Moreover, it gives a comprehensive summary of the various approaches taken by the Christian Churches in Africa at the present moment. The themes of "Prophetic Theology", "Black Theology", "African Theology" and the "Coping/Healing Churches" are treated in a competent matter and help to see the the Pastoral Plan of the Catholic Church in Southern Africa in its proper setting.

In the venture of inculturation, the central point is neither Evangelisation nor Context but the human person. In order to reach the heart of a people, the Church does not proceed from one "-ism" to another. The human person is the way of the Church. A special contribution of the Church in Africa may well be to bring into focus this scope of inculturation : not the development of an African humanism but the spiritual and holistic growth of African humanity: women, men and children fully African and fully Christian.

Arij A. Roest Crollius, S.J.

EVANGELISATION IN THE SOUTH AFRICAN CONTEXT

CONTENTS

CHAPTER ONE: INTRODUCTION

CHAPTER TWO: THREE EMERGING THEOLOGIES

CHAPTER THREE: TWO EMERGING PASTORAL RESPONSES

3.1 THE GROWTH OF THE COPING/HEALING CHURCHES.

  3.1.1 Introduction.

  3.1.2 The African Independent Churches.
       3.1.2.1 Healing in Traditional Zulu Culture.
       3.1.2.2 Healing in the African Independenc Churches.

  3.1.3 Coping/Healing in the "White" Neo-Pentecostal Churches.
       3.1.3.1 Appearance of the Phenomenon.
       3.1.3.2 Doctrine.
              3.1.3.2.1 The Doctrine of Classical Pentecostalism.
              3.1.3.2.2 Doctrine in The Charismatic Renewal.
              3.1.3.2.3 The "New" Independent Churches.
       3.1.3.3 The Coping/Healing Ministry in Pentecostalism and
                its Manifestation in the New Churches.

3.2 THE PASTORAL PLAN OF THE CATHOLIC CHURCH
     IN SOUTHERN AFRICA.

  3.2.1 Introduction: The Roots of the Pastoral Plan.

  3.2.2 The Pastoral Plan and its Theme.
       3.2.2.1 Community.
       3.2.2.2 Serving Humanity.

  3.2.3 The Pastoral Plan and its Method.

  3.2.4 Building Community: Three Methods Commended
         by the Pastoral Plan.
       3.2.4.1 Small Christian Communities.
       3.2.4.2 The "Renew" Method.
       3.2.4.3 Community Building Through Multiple Task Groups.

  3.2.5 Ongoing Training Methods.

  3.2.6 Conclusion.

CHAPTER FOUR: INTERPRETATION OF THE PHENOMENA:
THE SEARCH FOR A HERMENEUTIC KEY

CHAPTER FIVE: CONCLUSION

EVANGELISATION IN THE SOUTH AFRICAN CONTEXT

ABBREVIATIONS

AIC   African Independent Churches.

ANC   African National Congress.

Dom. Viv.   Dominum et Vivificantem (Encyclical Letter of Pope John Paul
            II on the Holy Spirit, May 18 1986).

EN   Evangelii Nuntiandi (Apostolic Exhortation of Pope Paul VI
            on Evangelization of the men of our time, December 8 1975).

ETSA   "Evangelisation Today in South Africa" Report to the SACBC
            1976.

GS   Gaudium et Spes (Pastoral Constitution on the Church in the
            Modern World: Vatican II).

LG   Lumen Gentium (Dogmatic Constitution on the Church:
            Vatican II).

NGK   Nederduitse Gereformeerde Kerk (Dutch Reformed Church).

SACBC   Southern African Catholic Bishops Conference.

SACC   South African Council of Churches.

WARC   World Assembly of Reformed Churches.

WCC   World Council of Churches.

UR   Unitatis Redintegratio (Decree on Ecumenism: Vatican II).

CHAPTER ONE

INTRODUCTION

1.1 Purpose of the Study.

> The people of God believes it is led by the Spirit
> of the Lord who fills the whole world. Moved by
> that faith it tries to discern in the events, the
> needs, and the longings which it shares with other
> men of our time, what may be genuine signs of the
> presence or of the purpose of God. [GS 11]

This famous quote from the "Pastoral Constitution of
the Church in the Modern World" of the Second Vatican
Council, indicates an imperative for the Church to search
for the will of God in the events of the time. The purpose
of this paper is to examine several phenomena which are
appearing at this time in South Africa. These phenomena are
considered to be "signs of the time" which the Church is
required to "read....and interpret... in the light of the
Gospel" (GS 4). From our examination, we hope to discover
what these phenomena are indicating regarding the priorities
for Evangelisation in the South African context today.
The signs we wish to consider have mainly appeared
since 1970 and form part of the response of Christians
within the various Churches to the prevailing social,
economic, political and cultural reality of South Africa.
We suggest that these signs can be described in terms of
five phenomena:

-The emergence of "Prophetic Theology".
-The emergence of "Black Theology".
-The emergence of "African Theology".
-The emergence and growth of the "Coping/Healing"
Churches aimed at helping people deal with the present
crisis situation.
-The emergence of a "Pastoral Plan" in the Catholic
Church.

It is our contention that these phenomena are
contextual manifestations of a single process in which the
Church is rooting itself in the South African soil thus
moving from being a "settler-mission" Church to a "local"
Church (de Gruchy 1979:1; Corijn 1987:1-2). This process
finds its source in the movement of the one Spirit and thus
carries important consequences regarding the unity of all
peoples and groups living in a divided South Africa. The
Local Church which is attempting to emerge is called to be

1

both a sign and sacrament of this unity (LG 1) and indeed of the emergence of a new South African culture. To the extent that the latter exists, this process is also one of Inculturation.

The first part of our study will be an attempt to present a description of each of the five phenomena as they are manifesting themselves within the South African context. Our sources for these descriptions will be the writings of various South African authors together with the intuitive vision which one acquires after twenty five years of life and seven years of pastoral ministry in the situation.

The second part of the study will attempt to interpret these phenomena in terms of a theological hermeneutic key. The search for this key will lead us to examine two interpretative models: that of Contextualisation and that of Inculturation. We will show that both models can be used to reveal complementary conclusions for Evangelisation in the South African context.

The emphasis of this work will be on the consequences of the phenomena studied on the process of Evangelisation. For some authors, Contextualisation and Evangelisation are almost synonymous (Cf. Padilla 1978:20). Others have made similar claims regarding Inculturation and Evangelisation (De Napoli 1987:72n). Whilst we do not entirely share these views, it is clear that the choice of interpretative keys which we have made also indicates the orientation that this work has towards the question of Evangelisation. Thus in our conclusion we hope to show some priorities for Evangelisation that the phenomena indicate.

Our choice of emphasis clearly indicates the orientation of our analysis and interpretation and we do not claim that these are by any means either exhaustive or comprehensive. Indeed, in a paper of this length it is impossible to enter into any real depth of analysis given the wide range of issues we wish to explore. Nevertheless, the reader will note that the section on Black Theology is disproportionately longer than the others and the analysis is more detailed. There are two reasons for this. The first relates to the greater difficulty that the author, a white person, has had in allowing this phenomenon to manifest itself to him. The second reason is perhaps more fundamental and concerns our contention that the Black Theology phenomenon provides the key, in a certain way, to the whole process. It is certainly the catalyst which has initiated the movement of the local Church into a review of its priorities and a renewal of its identity as we explain in the text (infra 1.4; 2.1.2; 2.2.3.1; 4.2).

1.2 Methodological Presuppositions.

1.2.1 Contextual Theology.

This work is an exercise in Contextual Theology. By Contextual Theology we understand the search for meaning and understanding within a particular experience of faith. This experience is local or contextual and thus the theology which emerges is a theology done locally. Contextual Theology helps Christians develop a faith which responds to the situation in which they find themselves (Lutzbetak 1981:39).

1.2.2 The Understanding of Church.

The ecclesial situation in South Africa is extremely complex with more than 4700 separate Churches serving the various Christian groupings (Villa-Vincencio 1988:31). We wish to clarify at the outset that we cannot limit our study to the Catholic Church. Only 10 percent of the population or 15 percent of Christians call themselves Catholic (Scholten 1983:240). Moreover the phenomena which we will discuss manifest themselves throughout the various Christian communities in South Africa. In a certain way they are factors which have impelled the Churches towards a vision of commonality and communality (Cf. UR 1).

We shall take as our point of departure the vision of the Christian family as expressed in Vatican II:

> All who have been justified by faith in baptism are incorporated into Christ; they therefore have a right to be called Christians, and with good reason are accepted as brothers [and sisters] by the children of the Catholic Church. [UR 3]

It is this family of Christian communities which form the context of our study and it is the faith experience of this family, seeking to understand and live its faith in South Africa, which forms the object of our study.

1.2.3 Philosophical Background.

Fuellenbach has observed that theologians "constantly make statements without ever coming to grips with their own philosophical presuppositions" (Fuellenbach 1988-1989:136). In order to at least speak to his observation, we wish to outline, at the beginning, three philosophical strands which will permeate this work.

1.2.3.1 Phenomenological Analysis.

In considering the data which will be presented in analyzing the five phenomena, it is the author's intention to adopt a phenomenological approach rather than a purely empirical one. The difference between the two is seen in the assertion of the value of phenomenological intuiting as a source of data (Spiegelberg 1982:682). This implies that not only the senses are seen as the source of information but also the standpoint and vision of the one(s) to whom the phenomena are manifesting themselves. The value of this approach lies in the ability of Phenomenology to overcome the subjective-objective distinction especially in the understanding of it given by Maurice Merleau-Ponty (Speigelberg 1982:541) as well as the attempt of Phenomenology to get at general manifestations, essences and universals through particular instances (eidetic intuiting, Cf. Spiegelberg 1982:697). Also important is the attempt of Phenomenology to understand the composition and relationship of essences in order to understand phenomena and their meaning[1] .

1.

Phenomenologists are not in full agreement regarding the admitted steps and processes of the Phenomenological method. Spiegelberg has, however, attempted to synthesise the major elements of the method. Our own analysis attempts to broadly follow this sequence without pretending to be rigorous in its application. Spiegelberg describes the method as follows (1982:682):

1. The Investigation of a Particular Phenomenon.

    a) Phenomenological Intuiting: opening the eyes, listening, reflecting, intuiting.

    b) Phenomenological Analysis: Tracing the elements and structure of the phenomenon.

    c) Phenomenological Description:
       -predication in terms of known classes
       -negative predication in terms of known classes
       -predication by metaphor and analogy.

2. Investigation of general essences (eidetic intuiting)

3. Apprehending essential relations amongst essences.

1.2.3.2 Historical Processes and Dialectic.

The key to understanding the manifestation of phenomena and processes in history owes a lot in this work to the Hegelian dialectic. This is particularly true with regard to the following:

1. A vision of history which has a purpose (telos) (Lavine 1984:227).
2. A communal vision of the Agent in history (Hegel's famous "volksgeist").

   Although the author does not accept the vision of the nation state as the true individual of history, the analysis of communities of faith in terms of the spirit of the people, understood as their culture, is at the basis of this work. This is not to negate the role of individuals in history. However this latter is not the formal object of this particular work.

3. The dialectical process and tendency of thought.

   It is accepted that the Hegelian dialectic in which every concept, as it is thought about, begins to show its limitation and pass over to its opposite, expresses a fundamental truth about the nature of thought (Levine 1984:210). The tension between Thesis and Antithesis is eliminated as the idea is thought through and elements of both are incorporated into a new understanding. This tool will be used in the paper in order to understand and interpret several of the phenomena and especially their development through history as well as their relationship, one to the other.

1.2.3.3 The Vision of Man Implicit in the Work.

Whilst it is clearly impossible to indicate a vision of man in just a few lines, we do consider it necessary to at least give some pointers concerning our presuppositions in this regard. Our anthropology is clearly a Christian one and we view man within the context of Revelation and the Tradition of the Community of Faith. Especially important in this regard, is the vision of *Gaudium et Spes* (GS 12-39).

Nevertheless, if there is an emphasis we have taken, we believe that it can be summed up in the oft quoted phrase of St. Irenaeus: "gloria enim Dei vivens homo" (Adv. Her. Lib. 4,20,7: SC 100,648). By this, we wish to affirm that

5

creation is fundamentally good and that this is particularly so for man since he is the image of God (GS 12). This foundation remains even after sin has been introduced, resulting in man's existential condition being one of division within himself (GS 13). Sin and death destroy life, but the new life that Christ brings is a freedom from sin and death. This freedom is a reality for man today not because of our own merits but through the glorification of God in Christ: the new man. This presents us with an eminently positive view of man redeemed in Christ and called to be fully alive, without denying the reality of evil and sin and the daily struggle against them.

Finally, we affirm that the locus of man's life is the world. He is Being-in-the-world and Being-with-others-in-the-world. Thus man is a cultural being where culture is understood in the sense of man's self realisation in his world together with others (Roest Crollius 1980: 259-263). In his world, man finds a goal which is salvation understood as the Kingdom of God and whilst there is a necessary rupture between the coming of the kingdom in its fullness and the world in which we live, there is also a necessary connection between the two. The Kingdom is already amongst us and at the same time, not yet fulfilled. Nevertheless, to the extent that Christ is present, incarnate, crucified and resurrected, in the world and in history then the Kingdom is present amongst us (Fuellenbach 1987:71-75). Man fully alive can then participate in the Kingdom today and Evangelisation implies the witness and proclamation of this truth (EN 33-35).

1.3   The Historical Context.

The historical development of the present Church situation in South Africa, can be understood in two different ways. The first of these considers a chronological ordering of events and an analysis of these events into epochs. The second is more concerned with the various forces, stresses and phenomena within the historical development of the Church and how these have influenced and determined the present situation. Corijn's analysis of the Catholic Church follows the first model (Corijn 1984:1), whereas de Gruchy's analysis follows the latter (de Gruchy 1979:1-52).

Corijn outlines four periods in the history of the Catholic Church in South Africa[2].

----

2. Corijn's analysis follows that of the Working Paper of the Pastoral Plan of the South African Catholic Bishops Conference (SACBC

1. Beginnings (1837-1870).
   In this initial phase the major concern of the Church was the small group of Catholic immigrants and soldiers. Three Vicariates were established: The Cape Vicariate in 1837, The Eastern Cape Vicariate in 1847 and the Natal Vicariate in 1850.

2. Consolidation and Growth (1870-1918).
   With the discovery of diamonds in 1867 and gold in 1886, there was a large influx of european immigrants and a strong growth in the economy. The Church was thus able to greatly expand its service to the local immigrant population during these years. At the same time a serious effort was made to begin the evangelisation of the local black population.

3. Expansion and Intensification (1918-1945).
   The number of ecclesial divisions increased from seven in 1918 to eighteen in 1945 and many new religious congregations arrived with the specific aim of evangelising the local black population. There was a strong reliance on the mission school as the principal means of contact with the people and the number of these schools increased considerably.

4. Emergence of the South African Church (1945-Today).
   In 1947, the Episcopal Conference of South Africa was set up and in 1948 the Afrikaner Nationalists swept into power. These two facts provide the framework for the emergence of the South African Church. In 1951 the South African hierarchy was established and soon began to issue statements and Pastoral Letters concerning the situation of the country. During this period there has also been a growing awareness that the first phase of evangelisation was over and since then more efforts have been placed on local vocations, seminaries and the development of a more localised Church.

1984:45-48). This document also gives an interesting historical overview of the sources of the present South African situation (1984:18-33) as well as a survey of attitudes within the various Churches (1984:34-48).

de Gruchy considers some of the particular elements of the historical process in the South Africa Churches which have had an influence on the situation today (de Gruchy 1979:1-52). One of these is the clash of interests between the "Settler Church" and the "Mission Church". The "Settler Church" was ministering to the needs of the white settlers, basically transporting the European model of Church to South Africa. The "Mission Church" was the fruit of the renaissance of mission endeavour which occurred during the 19th century (de Gruchy 1979:2). The missionaries who had come to evangelise and serve black communities were clearly more involved with the interests of their own members.

> The basic reason that Dutch and English settlers alike resented the presence of some missionaries was thus precisely because the missionaries not only evangelized the indigenous peoples, but took their side in the struggle for justice, rights and land. [de Gruchy 1979:13]

The notion of taking sides, a division of interests within and between the various Churches and Church groups remains essential for an understanding of the South African Christian context (Nolan 1988:199-200). It forms part of many of the phenomena we shall be studying in this work. It has also manifested itself in the black Church/ white Church division which forms part of the ecclesial development of the Churches during the 20th century (de Gruchy 1979:41).

Clearly, the major socio-political factor which has determined the morphology of the Christian community today in South Africa is the Apartheid policy of the government (de Gruchy 1979:53f). Nevertheless, it should be noted that this policy, adopted since 1948, is merely a more rigorous articulation of the beliefs, prejudices and practices of previous governments (de Gruchy 1979:54).

As the Churches have begun to root themselves in the local context and thus become a local Church, the nature of the Church has begun to change, together with its identity and preoccupations. This movement has accelerated in the last 20 years possibly due to the catalytic influence of four events:

1. The general spirit of change and renewal during the 1960's.
2. The effect of Vatican II on the Catholic Church in particular and, through a ripple effect, on the other Churches.
3. The re-examination of the missionary movement after the Uppsala conference of the World Council of Churches in 1968, and the Bangkok conference of 1973 leading to

the questioning of the necessity for missionaries and the call for a missionary moratorium (Anderson 1974:136-138).

4. The growth in importance of Contextual Theologies and in particular of Liberation Theology in Latin America and of Black Theology in the United States.

The process is only at its beginning and as late and 1976, a comprehensive research on the state of the Catholic Church in South Africa remarked that "the Catholic Church is not yet showing a typical South African Catholic tradition" (Hulsen 1976:21).

1.4 Recent Emergent Signs Amongst the Churches in South Africa.

During the same twenty year period of 1970 to 1990, it is possible to observe the emergence of several phenomena which are clearly linked to the rooting process referred to above. We contend that these phenomena are in fact the major manifestations of this process. The first of these is the emergence of "Prophetic Theology" as an attempt by Christians to present the demands of the Gospel to the leaders of society, to the rich and to the powerful. The leaders of the Churches within South Africa have to a greater or lesser extent, spoken out about various situations of injustice in the country. Whilst there are instances of this dating back to the 1930's[3], it is really since the Second World War that this ministry has become prominent. The concretisation of these ministerial statements into a formal theology has occurred during the 1980's with the decision to declare Apartheid a Heresy by, at first, the World Alliance of Reformed Churches, followed later by some other denominations (de Gruchy & Villa-Vicencio 1983:168-184). In 1985, the Kairos Document was released and with it, the characteristics of a Prophetic Theology for South Africa were first outlined[4].

Black Theology, as a discipline attracting a large number of black authors and proponents, has emerged in South Africa since the early 1970's. It is an attempt by black Christians, to reflect on their faith experience in an

----

3. Cf. for example the letter of Bishop Hennemans to the clergy of Cape Town in 1939 cited in SACBC 1985:217.

4. The Kairos Document: Challenge to the Church, Eerdmans, Grand Rapids, 1986. The background to this document and an analysis of its contents is given later (infra Chapter 2).

Apartheid society of which they are the victims. Black Theology is one of the large family of "Liberation" theologies and concerns itself primarily with social, economic and political categories.

Some authors in the Black Theology movement are becoming aware of the need to dialogue with non-black faith experiences using the categories of African thought and culture rather than Western ones (Tlhagale 1985:36). Consequently, African Theology as a theology concerned with the insertion of faith experience into African patterns of thought expression and culture is becoming more important. African Theology was previously considered to be little related to the situation in South Africa where the issues of dignity and liberation were still the priority (Cf. Ndebele 1972:26; Gqubule 1974:20). Now that the consciousness moment of Black Theology is yielding to the dialogue moment, African Theology is becoming more important (Kunnie 1986:153).

Linked with the above is the growing recognition of the importance of the African Independent Churches as a valid manifestation of African Christianity. Daneel maintains that: "Much of what we observe today in the Independent Churches concerns a genuinely contextualised and originally African response to the Gospel irrespective of and unfettered by mission Church influence" (1983a:58).

To the extent that this is true, the African Independent Churches would form part of the emerging phenomenon of African Theology. However it is our contention that these Churches form one half of a third emerging phenomenon in the South African ecclesial family.

Since 1979 the country has witnessed a phenomenal growth in the number of the so called "New Churches"[5]. These Churches are Fundamentalist and Pentecostal in nature and stress in particular the so called "prosperity message" that the Christian faith carries with it the right to material benefits. Together with the African Independent Churches, they form part of the emergence of what we will term a "Coping/Healing Ministry". By this we mean that these Churches are helping people to deal with the difficulties and problems they face by using the theological category of 'healing' in a particular way. In doing this they help people to cope with the stresses and fears resulting from living in a highly stressed society.

The first three phenomena we considered respond more to the issue of the identity of the Church, of its self understanding and of the content of its evangelisation. They

----

5. The term is adopted by Morran & Schlemmer (1984: iii) and is explained later in the text (infra Chapter 3).

are thus theologies: Prophetic Theology, Black Theology and African Theology. They are considered together in Chapter Two.

The phenomenon of the growth in the coping/healing ministry is more concerned with the pastoral practice of the Church. The final phenomenon we wish to consider is also one of pastoral practice. Here we will be concerned with the way in which the traditional Churches are responding to the challenge of the present time. We will limit ourself to the Catholic Church where, after a process of consultation and discussion lasting from 1974 to 1988, an initial three year campaign has been introduced throughout the Church as a "Pastoral Plan for the Catholic Church in Southern Africa" (SACBC 1989). This plan, which has the theme "Community Serving Humanity", lays its emphasis on restoring a sense of community to a society which is fragmented and divided. It's aim is to bring people together as serving Christian communities. Small Christian Communities are seen as the major vehicle for achieving this (SACBC 1987:20).

CHAPTER TWO
THREE EMERGING THEOLOGIES

2.1 PROPHETIC THEOLOGY.

In recent years, some South African authors have begun
to verify the emergence of a "Prophetic Theology" within the
South African Ecclesial family[6]. This theology calls itself
"Prophetic" because it addresses itself to a particular
socio-political context: the South African Apartheid
society, which it prophetically pronounces sinful in the
eyes of God. It's purpose is to articulate and express the
sinfulness of this context and then to announce a message of
salvation within it (Nolan 1986:139).

The proponents of this Prophetic message consider
themselves to be exercising a valid prophetic role of the
Christian community, expressing the will of God as it is
received by the community in faith (Shelp & Sutherland
1985:11).

The Prophetic Ministry of the Church forms part of its
identity as the community of faith (LG 12 Cf. Shelp &
Sutherland 1985:18&43). It is the community itself which is
prophetic (Shelp & Sutherland 1985:23). Those individuals
who articulate the prophetic role in magisterial,
ministerial and theological statements are individuals
called to speak in the name of the Christian community as it
hears God's word through its lived experience of faith.

Whilst this theology has only crystallized and been
named as such in the decade of the 1980's, it has its roots
further back in time and in order to understand the
phenomenon it is necessary to trace the history of its
appearance.

2.1.1 Post War Ecclesial Statements.

It has already been suggested that the post World War
Two period marks the beginning of the emergence of the
Christian Church in South Africa with a South African
character (supra 1.3). Concomitant to this process has been
the growing number of documents issued by the Magisterium
and leadership of the various Churches responding to various
situations in South African society in need of redemption.
Some of the most important of these documents are listed
below.

----

6. de Gruchy 1986:62-63, 81-95; Nolan 1986:131-140; Jacobs 1986:46-50
are examples of the many articles on the emergence of this phenomenon.

1948   Statements on the Race Issue[7].
1949 Rossetenville Ecumenical Conference document[8].
1957   SACBC "Statement on Apartheid"[9].
1961 Cottesloe Consultation Statement[10].
1968   SACC "Message to the people of South Africa"[11].
1972   SACBC Document "A Call to Conscience[12].

----

7. On the Introduction of Early Apartheid Legislation by the Newly
Elected Apartheid Government:Statements criticising the legislation:
   1948 Statement of the General Assembly of the Presbyterian Church.
   Statement of the Methodist Conference.
   Statement of the Baptist Union.
   Anglican "Statement on the Race Issue".

      Sources for footnotes 7-12 :
         Villa-Vicencio 1986:197-269.
         SACBC n.d.1, *The Bishops Speak Vol. I* . Pretoria.
         SACBC n.d.2, *The Bishops Speak Vol. II*. Pretoria.

8. This conference affirms the essential unity of all humanity and
affirms that the real need for South Africa is Unity and not Apartheid.

9. 1951 saw the erection of the South African Catholic Hierarchy.In
1952, the South African Catholic Bishops Conference issued their first
Statement on Race Relations. This statement affirms that discrimination
based exclusively upon colour is an offence against the rights of
non-Europeans and their dignity as human beings. The 1957 SACBC
"Statement on Apartheid" contains the first declaration by a Church that
Apartheid is "intrinsically evil".

10. The 1961 Cottesloe Consultation Statement.
   This meeting was attended by all the Churches including the white
   Afrikaans Reformed Churches. The occasion was the crisis brought
   about by the Sharpeville killings in 1960 and the subsequent
   banning of the ANC and imprisoning of its leaders including Nelson
   Mandela.
   The Conference adopted important resolutions including:
         -rejecting all unjust discrimination.
         -the spiritual unity of all men must find expression in
         common worship, witness and fellowship.
         -Concrete resolutions on issues such as:
            -justice in judicial processes.
            -freedom of worship.
            -migrant labour.
            -job reservation.

11. The 1968 South African Council of Churches
"Message to the People of South Africa".
   This important and controversial document attempts to show how
   Apartheid is contrary to the Gospel and how it denies the
   expression of the unity of mankind won by Christ. It also attempts
   to point out the hypocrisy in some Churches between what is said
   and the actual racial practice of the Church. It points out that
   obedience to God demands that the Church witness to unity in South
   Africa.

12. 1972 SACBC Document: "A Call to Conscience".
   The document, prompted by the 1971 Synod of Bishops on the theme

These early attempts of the predominantly english language Churches to react to the prevailing social context through statements directed at the conscience of the Government and of whites in general, formed the seeds of the emergence of a Prophetic Theology (de Gruchy 1986:82-83). They follow the style of the Old Testament Prophets with respect to three issues[13]:

> a) They indicate the particular social situation which is giving rise to concern. This is done by means of an accusation made to those responsible (Cf. Jer 22,13-17; Amos 4,1).
> b) they indicate God's displeasure with this situation.
> c) there is an exhortation to change the situation.

Many of these documents, whilst lacking the emotion of the Prophetic Scriptures tend to follow the same outline. One could thus say that there is a parallel to the judgement and salvation speeches the Prophets make to their own nation in the Prophetic books of the Old Testament (Westerman 1957:95). Whilst it would be anachronistic to take the parallel too far, the prophetic nature of these earlier statements is clearly present[14].

By the mid 1970's, the initiative and leadership within the Churches was passing from white into black hands[15]. The

----

of Justice, called Catholics to witness to social justice in the South African situation. It's aim was to inform and enlighten Christian consciences especially those of whites.

13. Cf. Scott:1968. The author gives an outline of the prophetic message and its composition. Cf. especially pp. 108-110, 112-113, 171-173 & 208-215.

14. Scott warns of the illegitimacy of transferring sayings of the Prophets from one cultural and religious context to another (1968:173). Here we are more concerned with looking at parallels of form to indicate the prophetic nature of the documents under consideration. Oden indicates that ministry today is linked with that of the Apostles and that the ministry of prophecy has continued to be important in the life of the Church. So, today, the Church is required to exercise a Prophetic ministry (1983:76f).

15. Before 1960, very few blacks held leadership positions within the traditional Church denominations. In 1951 there were no black bishops in the South African Catholic hierarchy. Even by 1971 there was only one out of a total of 30. By 1981 the position had improved and there were eight black bishops compared to four South African white bishops and thirteen foreign born bishops. (Source Authors Research). In the other Churches the situation is better but it was only in 1963 that Seth Mokitini became the first black leader of an english language Church in South Africa (Villa-Vicencio 1988:151).

Black Consciousness movement, events in the townships and growing numbers of blacks in Church leadership led to the growing disaffection with a liberal approach calling for a change in conscience and opened the way for a growing emphasis on the understanding of faith as praxis.

The first crisis that these changes provoked was the realisation that those Churches which had made such powerful statements denouncing the social evils of racism, unequal wealth distribution and Apartheid, were in fact infected within themselves with the same social evils. The actual practice within the Church conformed far more to the social reality it was condemning than it did to the witness called for by its leaders[16].

2.1.2 The Emergence of Prophetic Theology.

The realisation of the contradiction between the statements made in the name of the Churches and practice in the daily life of these same Churches has led to a demoralizing defensiveness and a loss of initiative within them. Villa-Vicencio has referred to them as being "Trapped in Apartheid" (1988:125 and the title of the book itself). The requirement to escape from this trap and to search for a new source of energy and vitality has rendered these Churches more open to the message of Black Theology as well as to new more authentic expressions of faith as lived by those who are the victims of oppression in society. The witness of more charismatic individuals becomes more important at this time and leaders emerge who through their Prophetic Witness to Gospel values in a crisis situation help call the Church to a new vision of its identity and mission[17].

The contact between the reality of the suffering Church and the experience of inauthenticity felt in the official Church has helped to deepen the notion and expression of Prophetic Theology which has thus emerged as a separate

----

16. Cf. Hulsen 1976:181-182; Kairos Doc. 1986:9-16; de Gruchy 1979:94; Jubber 1982:124f; Villa-Vicencio 1988:125.

17. Boesak points out that the Prophet comes along when the people are in crisis (Cf. Hab. 1,1-4). The Vision he presents is of the God of the Exodus who is the God of the Poor who will free his people from their slavery. He presents a vision of liberation realised in the sign of the Kingdom of God. Those who threaten the Prophet's vision are the High and Mighty, the arrogant and those who fear to be involved because they will lose their privileges (Boesak 1984:62-69). Clearly people such as Boesak himself, Archbishops Desmond Tutu and Denis Hurley as well as the Reverend Beyers Naude are performing this task in South Africa today.

phenomenon. This process has expressed itself in at least four major manifestations of Prophetic Theology during the 1980's:

The Proclamation of Apartheid as a Heresy (1982).
The Sanctions and Disinvestment Campaign (1983-1985).
The Kairos Document (1985).
The Call to Pray for the End to Unjust Rule in South Africa (1985).

2.1.2.1 The Proclamation of Apartheid as a Heresy.

The Southern African Catholic Bishops were the first Church leaders to identify Apartheid as "intrinsically evil" in their 1957 statement on Apartheid (de Gruchy & Villa Vicencio 1983:144). In 1968 the South African Council of Churches condemned it as a "false Gospel" (1983:145).

Nevertheless, it was at the meeting of the World Alliance of Reformed Churches in Ottawa in 1981 where Apartheid was declared sinful and the theological and moral justification of it to be a heresy (de Gruchy & Villa-Vicencio 1983:xi). This decision was taken as the result of an address delivered by the Reverend Allan Boesak, a minister of the Nederduitse Gereformeerde Sendingkerk[18]. In his address, he asked that the World Association of Reformed Churches reaffirm racism as a sin and Apartheid as a heresy as enunciated in the document of the Association of Black Reformed Christians of Southern Africa in 1981 (de Gruchy & Villa-Vicencio 1983:1-9, 161).

Since then several Ecclesial bodies in South Africa have adopted resolutions embracing this affirmation. Both the Methodist and Anglican Churches did so in 1982 with other Churches following later (de Gruchy & Villa-Vicencio 1983:145).

----

18. The Dutch Reformed Church in South Africa is structured along racial lines. The "Nederduitse Gereformeerde Kerk" is the white Mother Church. It has given birth to three mission Churches: The "Nederduitse Gereformeerde SendingKerk in Suid Afrika", The "N.G.K. in Afrika" and the "Reformed Church in Africa". These Churches have been constituted as racial Churches serving different racial groups. The "Nederduitse Gereformeerde Sendingkerk" was constituted in 1881 and is for so called "Coloured" or "mixed race" people. The "NGK in Afrika" was established in 1963 as a Church serving black members. The "Reformed Church in Africa" serves those of Asian origin and was also established during the 1960's.
Source: Heyns 1986:764-766.

2.1.2.2 The Sanctions and Disinvestment Campaign.

The judgement oracle of prophetic utterance in the Scriptures normally contains an indictment and a sentence which is the sanction resulting from sinful behaviour (Scott 1968:109). These sanctions were normally carried out through the historico-political process of the time which was then interpreted in prophetico-theological categories (Cf.Blenkinsopp 1969:37). God is seen to act within history and history can be interpreted in terms of his presence (Scott 1968:160-161; 164-170).

The categories of Indictment and Punishment/Sanction form the theological basis of the Disinvestment and Sanctions Campaign[19]. The roots of this paradigm can be found in the World Council of Churches call for economic and military sanctions against South Africa in 1968. But it is only during the 1980s with the call for non-violent, effective forms of coercion on the South African Government made by black Christians, especially Allan Boesak and Archbishop Desmond Tutu, that the issue has become pertinent in the Christian community and the nation as a whole (Villa-Vicencio 1988:117).

----

19. The Catholic Bishops have indicated the following different types of Economic Pressure

1. Divestment
    This is a process whereby pressure is put on bodies to withdraw funds from companies which are investing in South Africa, for example, by selling shares in companies operating in the country. The aim is to put pressure on big business and the government to change. Divestment helps to expose the horrors of Apartheid and to create a lack of confidence in the system at international level.

2. Disinvestment:
    This has a number of aspects such as refusing new capital investment in South Africa, withdrawing or refusing loans, selling existing plants and removing physical capital.

3. Embargoes and Trade Sanctions:
    Banning trade with South Africa either export or import.

4. Boycotts:
    Similar to sanctions but can also be applied by non-governmental persons or agencies.

Source: SACBC 1986, *Pastoral Letter on Economic Pressure for Justice.* Mariannhill.

The Catholic Church has probably reflected more at length on this issue than the other Churches especially in their document "On Economic Pressure for Justice". The prophetic dimension is clearly alluded to in this document. The Bishops refer to this deliberation and the fruits thereof as: "The prophetic task [which] demands of us that we reflect on the issue in the light of the Gospel" (SACBC 1986:1); "...a prophetic witness..." (SACBC 1986:2) and "This prophetic calling that requires us...to make a direct intervention in the affairs of the country" (SACBC 1986:3). In their conclusion to the document the Bishops indicate their belief "that economic pressure has been justifiably imposed to end apartheid...[and] that such pressure should continue and if necessary be intensified" (SACBC 1986:4).

2.1.2.3 The Call to Pray for an End to Unjust Rule.

Prayer for the leaders of the nation has always formed part of the Christian liturgy and finds its roots in many biblical injunctions (Cf. 1 Tim. 2,1-2). In 1985, the document "A Theological Rationale and a Call for the end to Unjust Rule" was produced by the South African Council of Churches. The document requested Christians to pray that "God in His Grace may remove from His people....the present rulers in our country who persistently refuse to heed the cry for justice...." (Villa-Vincencio 1986:249).

The call met with much reluctance on the part of many Churches and their leaders. Whilst their apparant theological vision proclaimed the right to pray for enlightenment and change on the part of the Government, the clearly confrontational nature of the call appeared to be too much for them and almost all stopped short at organizing prayer services for an end to unjust rule as called to do so by the SACC (Villa-Vicencio 1988:153-158). In this way, the Church was forced to confront the issue of whether to always accept and pray for those in government, as Romans 13 seems to suggest, or whether or not it is possible for the Church to commit itself to the removal of those in office when their conduct merits it, at least through recourse to prayer.

2.1.2.4 The Kairos Document.

With the publication of this document in September 1985, the category known as Prophetic Theology was given form and content within the South African context. The Kairos Document is a 35 page booklet divided into six chapters. The first chapter sets the tone by indicating that a "Kairos" - a particular moment of truth - has arrived for South Africa and that this has important consequences for the South African Church. The next three chapters describe three theologies present in South Africa at this time. "State Theology" is criticised as the ideology which the State uses to legitimate it's own position. The document denounces the god of this Theology as an idol similar to those of the false gods of the court Prophets of Israel (Kairos Doc. 1986:8). "Church Theology" is also criticised as the manifestation of a particular kind of spirituality and religion which does not wish to be involved in the political and social life of people. According to the document, "Church Theology" manifests itself in the call for reconciliation where there has been no confession of sin and repentance as well as in calls for non violence and justice which see no need to change the basic status quo of the society. "Prophetic Theology" is presented as the response in faith which is required by the present Kairos. It is a theology which concerns itself with the social context of the People of God. The final two chapters of the document are a challenge to action and a conclusion calling for further reflection on these issues. Arguably the most Controversial dimension of this document was the critique of "Church Theology" and whilst this part of the document has been criticized as being too narrow and a little unfair, the document's frame of reference is nevertheless clear as its title proclaims it a "Challenge to the Church"[20]. Its clarity in unmasking the difference between theory and practice in the official English language Churches has challenged them to liberate themselves from this contradiction. In this way it has laid the groundwork for a new step in faith. For the document itself, this new step is Prophetic Theology.

2.1.3 Prophetic Theology in the Kairos Document.

The Kairos Document outlines seven characteristics of a Prophetic theology (Kairos Doc. 1986:17-18):

It is biblical.
It reads the "signs of the times".
It is a call to action.

----
20. The Kairos Document was produced by a group of theologians who began meeting in June 1985 in an attempt to reflect on the growing crisis within the country and to draw up a document which would provide a vision of where the Church was called to move. The first edition of the document was released in September 1985. The comments here are based on the second revised edition published in 1986 (Cf. Kairos Doc. 1986).

It is always confrontational.
It emphasises hope.
It is spiritual.
It is pastoral in that it
 -denounces sin by naming the sins and evils of the
 time.
 -announces salvation, understood both as future
 liberation, justice and peace, as being God's will
 for South Africa.

Fundamental to all of these, however, is the concept of the "Kairos" to which the document owes its name. The Kairos is the condition for the possibility of a Prophetic Theology. Albert Nolan, one of the signatories of the document has analysed this concept at some length[21]. For Nolan, Prophetic Theology is distinguished from other theologies or modes of theology by its characteristicly "time-bound" nature (1986:131). Following Von Rad (1968:100), he describes Kairos as "time as a quality". This understanding of time was common in Hebrew culture and is meaningful also in African culture. It is different to the quantified concept of time as "Chronos" common in Western understanding. "In the Bible the Prophet was someone who could tell the time...the Prophets could read the signs of the times...see what kind of time it was and what kind of action would be appropriate now" (Nolan 1986:134). This understanding of time is fundamental to the aim and purpose of the Kairos Document. Prophetic Theology is quintessentially Contextual Theology since times change.

Even more fundamental than the above is the fact that the Prophet was able to find God in the Kairos (Nolan 1986:134). Indeed in a certain way the Prophet is the manifestation or actualization or sacrament of the divine Kairos: a time in which God manifests himself in a particular way in a particular historical situation. In this time, He "visits his people to offer them a unique opportunity for repentance and conversion for change and decisive action" (Kairos Doc. 1986:33n1). History for Nolan is a "succession of God inspired events" and the Prophet is the one who has the ability to recognize these events and the presence of God within them.

The fundamental thesis of the Kairos Document is that such a "God event" is upon us now in South Africa. "It is the Kairos...not only for apartheid but also for the Church and all other faiths and religions" (Kairos Doc. 1986:1).

----
21. Nolan 1987:61-69; Nolan 1988:14-19; Nolan 1986:131-140.

2.1.3.1 A Prophetic Theology is Biblical.

Prophetic Theology requires a "return to the Scriptures to search the Word of God for a message that is relevant for what we are experiencing in South Africa today" (Kairos Doc. 1986:17). A Prophetic Theology is a theology of the Kairos and thus it considers only that part of the Word of God which speaks to the Kairos. It is the ability to discern what that Word is which gives it its prophetic character.

2.1.3.2 A Prophetic Theology reads the "Signs of the Times".

Prophetic Theology attempts to analyse the Kairos. This analysis concerns the prevailing social and economic situation. It tries to see what is happening in peoples lives and why, in an attempt to explain these events in terms of the Gospel (Kairos Doc. 1986:17; Cf. GS 4).

2.1.3.3 A Prophetic Theology is a Call to Action.

Prophetic Theology implies a call to respond in action to the prevailing situation and to the Kairos. The action is determined through a process of reflection and judgement on the situation, in the light of the Word of God indicated above (Kairos Doc. 1986:17-18; Cf. GS 43).

2.1.3.4 A Prophetic Theology is always Confrontational.

Prophetic Theology attempts to expose what is evil and what is sin in the prevailing situation and calls people to recognise and confront the sin and evil in which they are caught. Thus it rejects the reconciliation proposed by "Church Theology" since this is seen to be a compromise with evil (Kairos Doc. 1986:18; Cf. GS 13).

2.1.3.5 A Prophetic Theology emphasises Hope.

Prophetic Theology directs towards the future about which it has a message of good news in hope. Nolan points out that the notion of Kairos is "itself determined by its relationship to another kind of time: Eschaton" (Nolan 1987:63). It is the eschaton understood as "time-as-ultimate" or "final" which determines the nature of Kairos. Kairos is always open to Eschaton because it points

the way to Eschaton (Nolan 1987:66). These two are
paralleled again and again in the Scriptures in saying such
as "the time has come, the end is near; the time has come,
the day of Yahweh is near" (Nolan 1987:66). Thus the coming
of the Kairos implies the coming of hope that God will
reveal himself and establish His will. Prophetic Theology
tries to orient itself in this hope (Kairos Doc. 1986:18).

2.1.3.6 A Prophetic Theology is Spiritual.

The prophetic call is a call to the values of the
Spirit and not to those of the flesh. Anger, vengeance,
hatred, all of which are easily raised by a spirit of
confrontation, must give way to fearlessness, courage, love,
understanding, and joy as the values motivating action
(Kairos Doc. 1986:18).

2.1.3.7 A Prophetic Theology is Pastoral.

Prophetic Theology does not remain abstract. It
denounces sin by naming the specific evils of the specific
situation. In indicating the evils which exist in the
society, it wishes to inaugurate a program of searching for
ways in which the society can rid itself of these evils. By
similarly proclaiming the values and hopes upon which a new
society should be formed, it wishes to announce salvation to
people through a practical pastoral programme of action
(Kairos Doc. 1986:18).

2.1.4 Further Dimensions of Prophetic Theology in Souṭṇ Africa and its Impact Elsewhere.

We have not exhausted the themes of Prophetic Theology
in this short exposé. Other issues such as, for example, the
conscription of whites into military service, conscientious
objection to military service, the issue of violence and the
criteria for a just war in South Africa, also form part of
its content. What we have attempted to do here is to show
that Prophetic Theology is primarily aimed at confronting
the powers of the Land. Its addressees are primarily those
in authority and White South Africa in general. It thus
follows the direction established by the earlier statements
of the Churches against Apartheid and the prevailing social
conditions. It is the reverse coin of Black Theology. This
is true even though it has been Black Theology, and its
challenges, which have breathed life into this strand of
reflection on faith experience, leading to the birth of

Prophetic Theology as such. Indeed some of the Black Theology authors, especially Allan Boesak, refer to Black Theology as a Prophetic Theology (1977:14). Nevertheless, Prophetic Theology is particularly, although not totally, an exercise in White liberation. It is probably for this reason that the Kairos document has had such a wide impact in the Churches of the first world[22].

Today, the Liberation Theologies are challenging and demanding a response from the first world (Bucher 1976:518-534). The response has been in two directions: a reactionary response negating any value in Liberation Theology and a more positive one, accepting the challenge that it poses by attempting to search for a Liberation Theology for the oppressor[23].

There is no doubt that Prophetic Theology in South Africa stands within what Walter Brueggeman has called the "liberation trajectory" or Mosaic tradition of the Covenant (de Gruchy 1986:63). de Gruchy argues that in the New Testament, two prophetic streams can be identified: The Prophetic Ministry of Jesus himself and the Prophetic Ministry of the early Christian Community. He maintains that this vital dimension of the Church's life has been constantly present often as an uncomfortable presence in uneasy relationship with the institutional Church and its leaders who were not afraid to sometimes suppress it (1986:73f). The Church, in fact, needs the prophetic dimension to ensure its own authenticity since the Prophets denounce the compromises and rationalisations that men are wont to make in order to ensure an easy life.

> The Church today, in its mission to the world and in its own pastoral practice, has to discover how vital prophecy is to its own life and social praxis...The word of prophecy is addressed first of all to the community of faith...A church which is open to the Prophetic word of the Lord is a church

----

22. Solle suggests that South Africa provides a mirror of first world/ third world relations which renders a document such as the Kairos document full of international implications (1987:122). Its impact has certainly been overwhelming. Solle refers to it as of a "status which can scarcely be overestimated" (1987:116). It has been translated into many languages and debated in discussion groups throughout Europe and North America. See also World Council of Churches Document: *P.C.R. Information, Special Issue "Challenge to the Church"*. Geneva: WCC, n.d. for a selection of articles on the document.

23. Many books and articles are currently available presenting both sides of the argument. Buchers article gives an overview of the situation in 1976 (1976:517-534). McElvaney (1980) and Walsh (1982) give a positive appraisal of this influence whereas McCann (1981) is more critical. Solle's comments in Concilium 192(1987) are also important in this regard.

which is willing to allow itself to be caught up by the Spirit into the Messianic ministry of the crucified Lord to the world. [de Gruchy 1986:75-78]

Thus Prophetic Theology, and Prophetic Witnessing are quintessentially Evangelisation: evangelisation to the Church, and evangelisation by the Church to the world.

It is above all [Jesus'] mission and his condition of being an evangelizer that [the Church] is called upon to continue.... The Church is an evangelizer, but she begins by being evangelized herself...she has a constant need of being evangelized....in order to proclaim the Gospel.... Having been sent and evangelized, the Church herself sends out evangelizers. [EN 15]

The parallel between the two texts quoted illustrates to what extent the Prophetic Ministry of the Church is in fact evangelisation. The Pope goes on to affirm that "evangelization cannot but include the prophetic proclamation of a hereafter.... in both continuity and discontinuity with the present situation" (EN 28). This involves "an explicit message, adapted to the different situations constantly being realised, about the rights and duties of every human being,.....about life in a society, about international life, peace and justice and development - a message especially energetic today about liberation" (EN 29).

2.2 BLACK THEOLOGY.

2.2.1 Introduction.

During the 1970's, Black Theology began to emerge as a new phenomenon in South Africa. Since then it has played a major role within the South African Christian Community and necessarily forms part of this phenomenological analysis. Since Black Theology is a theology rooted in the black experience, this author admits that as a white, the phenomenon has to make a long journey outside its horizon of understanding in order to speak to him. Nevertheless, many black and some white authors have stated that this journey forms part of the purpose of Black Theology[24].

2.2.2 Towards a Definition.

Black Theology is not understood in the same way by all its authors. Indeed, there are differences of opinion concerning its starting point, purpose, limits, context and content. Despite these differences, there is still much common ground between the authors in this field. As our starting point we take the definition of Allan Boesak:

> Black Theology is the theological reflection of Black Christians on the situation in which they live and on their struggle for liberation. Blacks ask: what does it mean to believe in Jesus Christ when one is black and living in a world controlled by white racists? And what if these racists call themselves Christian too? [Boesak 1977:1-2]

Black Theology is thus situational and the situation is South Africa now. This leads to the question of the transient nature of Black Theology which for some is also a question about its authenticity (Ngubane 1986:89). For other authors the authenticity of Black Theology lies precisely in its situational nature (Biko 1978:59).

This leads to another area of conflicting opinions which concerns the question of priority in the process of theological reflection. For many authors, the priority factor in Black Theology is the black experience (Mosala 1986:183; Goba 1986b:66). Others see the starting point in God, His Word and the call to faith which "transcends

----
24. Boesak 1984:17; de Gruchy 1979:169; Tlhagale 1985:122; Boesak 1977:145; Maimela 1986:102-105.

specific groups and nations" (Boesak 1977:121). Here, the role of Black Theology is "to bring this message to our people" (Boesak 1984:27; Cf. also Dwane 1981:30). Mosala understands this problem as a conflict around the question of the universal and the particular (1986:183). He sees Black Theology as a particular theology for a particular situation. The situation is the starting point and influences what part of the Scripture becomes Word of God (1986:179-180). He accuses some Black Theologians of the application of universal principles found in the Word of God to particular situations, a process he considers to be rooted in the same "bourgeois theology" that Black Theology seeks to criticise (1986:180).

Black Theology situates itself clearly within the family of Liberation Theologies. It understands that black people in South Africa are oppressed because they are black. It also posits that God, who created them black, is opposed to the situation of oppression, which is sin, and will free them from it (Boesak 1977:16-19). Thus Christ the Liberator, understood by some authors as the Black Messiah, is central to Black Theology (Boesak 1977:41).

Black Theology has both a critical dimension and a positive dimension. Its critical role is oriented towards the praxis of the Christian community especially as it manifests itself in the creation, maintenance, indifference towards, or even support of, the present social system in South Africa and its roots in Apartheid. It is also critical of "White Theology" which it sees as a deformation of the Christian message[25]. Its positive dimension is oriented towards a lasting theology of man using African categories of understanding and culture (Motlhabi 1986:48). It is here that Black Theology comes closest to being African Theology and the relationship between these two is the source of much debate (infra 2.2.4.4.3 and 2.3.2.).

----

25. "White Theology is the name given to the theology which is seen to underpin and justify, the present situation in South Africa. It is a theology which speaks about Western Values and the importance of maintaining Christian civilization understood as the civilization brought by the whites to South Africa. Maimela, in his article "Man in White Theology" (1981:27-43) has produced a scathing indictment of the anthropology behind this theology considering it both unbiblical and pessimistic in its vision of man.
The term "White Theology" is used by other Black Theology authors to refer to Western theology in general and especially that part of it which considers itself universal (Cf. Echols 1984:27-31).

2.2.3 The Emergence of Black Theology.

2.2.3.1. The situation.

Black theology began to emerge in the early 1970s in South Africa and is in many ways the fruit of the situation at that time (Mosala & Tlhagale 1986:v). During the decade of the 1960's, many new countries were born as the decolonization process moved into full stride. In South Africa, however, the "winds of change"[26] did not blow and it became clear that change was not going to occur as a result of the devolution of power, but rather as the result of the efforts of the people themselves to win it (Cf. Goba 1986b:58, 67; Maimela 1986:102). Liberalism and paternalism were seen to have failed in this context. The struggles and disbanding of the Liberal Party in South Africa and the ineffectiveness of N.U.S.A.S. (National Union of South African Students), the two major liberal organisations in South Africa during the 1960's, bore witness to this failure (Biko 1978:156). It thus became clear that the black people of South Africa were going to have to win their liberation for themselves (Biko 1978:91).

Initially, the Black Consciousness movement, through S.A.S.O.[27], provided the vehicle for black intellectuals to formulate the vision for a new programme. But it was the decision of the University Christian Movement, a predominately black group with predominately white leadership, to set up a Black Theology project, which led to the emergence of Black Theology as a discipline in South Africa. The movement was quickly the focus of Government attention and, first, the director of the project was banned[28], followed by the president of the University

----

26. The phrase "winds of change" results from a speech made by Harold MacMillan, a former prime minister of Great Britain, in Cape Town in 1961 in which he described the decolonization of Africa and the birth of so many new states using this term.

27. S.A.S.O. (The South African Students Organisation) formed as a grouping of students at black universities (Universities were racially segregated by by law in 1957) during the late 1960's in order to reflect on their particular situation, their needs and aspirations (Biko 1978:3-7).

28. "Banning in South Africa refers to the restrictions placed on a person by the government which restricts them in various ways. This is done by decree of the Minister in terms of the Act and without any recourse to judicial process.
> The restriction orders or bans vary in their scope, but most commonly people are prevented from attending any gatherings and are restricted to their homes from dusk to dawn and all weekend. Banned people are generally prevented from carrying

Christian Movement (Motlhabi 1988:71). By 1972 the movement was to be subjected to a government enquiry and decided to disband just before this began. Before this, however, it was able to conduct a series of seminars on Black Theology throughout the country and from this the book "Essays in Black Theology" was published, the first fruit of the new theology (de Gruchy 1979:154). This book was subsequently published internationally under several different titles (Moore 1973).

2.2.3.2 The Roots of Black Theology.

In this section we hope to describe Black Theology in terms of an analysis of its three main roots: Black Consciousness, The Black Experience and Black Theology in the United States. We hope to show what it has abstracted from each of these roots in order to determine its own identity.

2.2.3.2.1 The Black Consciousness Movement.

Steve Biko defines Black Consciousness as:

The realisation by the black man of the need to rally together with him brothers around the cause of their operation - the blackness of their skin - and to operate as a group in order to rid themselves of the shackles that bind them to perpetual servitude. [1978:49]

Concerning its purpose he writes: "What Black Consciousness seeks to do is to produce...real black people who do not regard themselves as appendages to white society" (1978:51).

The movement is presented as the antithesis to the situation prevailing in the country which is interpreted as white racism. Faced with this the only response is the forging of a strong sense of black unity. The confrontation between Thesis and Antithesis will result in a synthesis which is a transforming moment: a South Africa where black and white can live together in mutual respect, harmony and interaction[29]   (Biko 1978:51).

----

out their jobs.... The banning order is renewable so that any person may be restricted for much longer than the original order. [Mermelstein 1987:91-92]

29. Black Consciousness has two basic moments to it. The first is an existential moment in which black people come to an awareness of their own dignity as black people created black by God

Takatso Mofokeng sees in Black Theology, a deliberate attempt by the Black Consciousness movement to develop a theology based on the categories and praxis of Black Consciousness (1986:22). If this is so then Black Consciousness becomes the "sine qua non" and major root of Black Theology. Bonganjalo Goba, however, understands Black Consciousness and Black Theology as two parallel movements arising out of, the same black experience of oppression, which is reflected upon in terms of different categories: Black Consciousness in ideological ones and Black Theology in religious ones (Goba 1986b:60-62). Since both movements are directed towards the aim of liberation, they are intertwined: "soul mates" (Goba 1986b:63). Motlhabi, combining the two, sees Black Theology as the "logical result and religious counterpart of Black Consciousness" (1986b:44).

2.2.3.2.2 The Black Experience in South Africa.

There is consensus that it is the particular situation under which people live in South Africa which gives Black Theology its existence and its specificity, in other words: its identity. This situation is very difficult for a white person to describe since one has to do so from outside and the experience loses its power. One can say that it is an experience of oppression: of being crushed[30]. Black peoples' lives are controlled from outside by a White Government, which considers them a danger[31], a problem: the race

----

(Goba 1986b:59; Cf. Motlhabi 1988:48). It is the moment in which "blackness" is held up as the ideal, the positive to be attained and integrated: "black is beautiful". It is a search for identity and authenticity. "We speak about a rebirth, a recreation, a re-evaluation of ourself" (Boesak 1984:16). This moment required isolation and separation on the part of blacks and led to the uninformed accusation by other groups that the movement was racism in reverse (Motlhabi 1988:49).

The second moment is a more extroverted one. It is the moment of encounter with the thesis: white racism, and of the transformation. This is the political category of Black Consciousness in which it seeks to transform society by the various means open to it. This is the moment of the "struggle" (Goba 1986b:59-63).

30. The understanding of oppression as being crushed is rendered well in the local African languages. Thus the zulu verb to be oppressed (ukucindezeka) carries this meaning of being pressed down; a concept close to the biblical understanding and present even in the latin but lost in the present english understanding of the word.

31. The term "Swart Gevaar" (Black Danger) has been used in the white political arena with great success. Its aim has been to frighten whites into following the policies of the ruling party.

problem, and non citizens of the country, since South Africa is considered to be a white man's country (Mermelstein 1987:3-4). It is a situation in which black people are considered barbaric, primitive, uncivilised and dangerous by whites in general. It is a situation in which the Government enacts all kinds of legislation to control and subjugate black people in terms of the various idealistic visions of social engineering and manipulation which take little account of the individuals, families and small groupings of people involved. These factors have evolved into the "Grand Apartheid" vision and policy[32]. The consequence has been the erection of social forms which mitigate against human dignity, creativity, freedom, tradition, culture and hope. It is the responsibility of Black Theology to relate this experience to the experience of God.

> This is the situation in which black people find themselves. Slavery, domination, injustice; being forced to live a life of contradiction and estrangement in their own country and "in exile," where fear and the urge to survive make deception a way of life; being denied a sense of belonging; discrimination - all these were realities which have almost completely broken down the sense of worth of black personhood. [Boesak 1976:29]

This is the experience which forms the basis of Black Theology as Boesak indicates in a later article: "Black Theological reflection must take seriously what Christian Theologians have hitherto ignored: the Black situation"(1977:10).

Steve Biko had already in 1972 pointed out this fundamental task of Black Theology as follows: "Black Theology...seeks to relate the present day black men to God within the given context of the black man's suffering and his attempt to get out of it" (1978:59).

S.S. Maimela points out that even within the Churches, which are almost all at least 80% black, the control, the vision and the modus operandi remain white. The Black Church is the "Church of the underclass": the poor, the workers, the unemployed and dominated women. Yet the theology of the

----

32. Apartheid is popularly divided into two forms. Grand Apartheid refers to the vision of the ruling Nationalist Party incarnated in the laws of residential and political separation. Petty Apartheid refers to the racial separation of public facilities such as buses, beaches, shops, cinemas and restaurants. The latter form of Apartheid is currently being dismantled in terms of the "Reform" process. The former remains currently (Jan 1990) untouched.

Churches is often oriented towards middle class values and experiences and thus even within the Church, blacks experience alienation and denial of their human reality (1988:16).

2.2.3.2.3 Black Theology in the United States.

There has always been a relationship between the Black Church in South Africa and that of the United States. Many of the African Independent Churches in South Africa can trace their roots to the United States. Other Churches have also been influenced by the cross pollination of ideas resulting from the visits South Africans have made to the United States and to a lesser extent through black Americans who have been able to visit South Africa.

It was thus obvious that the Black Consciousness movement and the Black Theology movement, once they had begun to emerge, would look to the black struggle for civil liberties in the United States for ideas and inspiration. The two movements are clearly different. The black struggle in the United States has been concerned with a minority of the population being able to actualise the civil rights already available to them in terms of the Constitution and Law of the United States. In South Africa, the struggle is of the majority of the people who are attempting to obtain the human rights effectively denied to them by the law (Mermelstein 1987:3). Despite these fundamental differences, parallels obviously exist between the two situations.

Black Theology in the United States was first given coherent form by James Cone with the publication of his works "Black Theology and Black Power" in 1969 and "A Black Theology of Liberation" in 1970. In the latter book he identifies six sources of Black Theology: the black experience, black history, black culture, revelation, Scripture, and tradition (Motlhabi 1986b:41). For Cone the inspiration of Black Theology is Scripture and especially Luke 4,18 which he calls the liberatory creed of Black Theology (Motlhabi 1986b:41).

American Black Theology continues to play a role in South African Black Theology. Indeed, Mokgethi Motlhabi contends that "Black Theology in South Africa as a discipline is a non-starter...American Black Theologians have advanced far ahead of us" (1986b:38), an opinion which he admits is not shared by all. For Goba, the link between the two is not fully clear. He maintains the contemporaneity of the civil rights movement in the United States and Black political awakening in South Africa and relates how "we discovered in [Cone's] theological hermeneutic, a fresh approach in engaging in the liberation struggle in our situation within an ecclesiastical situation." He goes on to readily acknowledge the domination of Cone's ideas in the development of South African Black Theology but he suggests that the relationship is more symbolic than anything else because of the different political situations (1986b:62).

2.2.4 The Context of Black Theology.

2.2.4.1 The Socio-Political Context.

The socio-political context of Black Theology is the Apartheid State of South Africa. Black Theology is fundamentally a reaction against the life-style that this socio-political context imposes upon Black people. It is an attempt to question the life-style people are coerced into in terms of the Gospel and the faith experience of the people. Black Theology has identified this socio-political context as "the system"[33] . The role of Black Theology is to oppose the "system" following the vision provided by the Kingdom of God. Consequently it looks for ways to transform the present situation in accordance with the guiding vision. When it does this then Black Theology becomes a Liberation Theology.

2.2.4.2. The Racial Context of Black Theology.

It may seem tautologous to consider race as a context for Black Theology but in fact the debate on the respective roles of race and class in the South African situation is one which has most divided the anti-government opposition forces. The Black Theologians say that the class analysis of society based on Marxist categories and used as a model for understanding South African society and thus as an indicator of a way out of the situation, does not sufficiently take into account the particularities of South Africa[34] .

----

33. "Apartheid and all it stands for is not the system that places its fortunes on the political judgement of a people. It demands, with idolatrous authority, a subservience and obedience in all spheres of life that a Christian can only give to God" (Boesak 1984:23; Cf. also Boesak 1984:112;).

34. See Sebidi (1986:14-22) for a discussion on the two positions and a conclusion that race is the fundamental context for Black Theology whilst the Marxian class analysis is considered a fad which divides the black opposition.

Through the process of reflecting critically on what it means to be oppressed and dominated, black people become the subject of their own history and their own theology (Maimela 1988:21). This reflection is: "the affirmation of our blackness ... it has nothing to do with being resigned to our blackness ... It is ... the affirmation of our creation as black" (Boesak 1984:15-16)[35].

2.2.4.3 The Cultural Context.

As black people have embarked upon the process of becoming the subject of their own theology it has become increasingly clear to them that the way in which Christianity has been presented to them is in many ways foreign to their own understanding. The religious and social systems set up in South Africa in the name of Christianity have often been ones of oppression. These systems have often been legitimised by theological arguments and positions clearly aimed at maintaining white privilege (Maimela 1988:21).

This has led to the search for new categories of understanding and new ways of expressing theological truths. This search has led to an investigation of the categories of African culture and anthropology, black history and the experience of suffering[36].

----

35. Bonganjalo Goba emphasises that Black Theology only emerges out of the black experience of this reality. Many people are oppressed throughout the world. In South Africa, oppression is formally linked to skin colour. "What must be emphasised is that Black Theology expresses itself within the context of our experience of oppression" (1986b:58).

Many people experience oppression throughout the world, but what is specific for Goba is that in South Africa, it is race which is determinant of the experience of oppression and therefore of the concomitant theology. "What distinguishes the political reality of our situation from others in the world is that we are oppressed first and foremost because we are black. This is a fundamental truth that even my own mother understands" (Goba 1986b:66).

36. S. Dwane outlines the process as follows: "As we decolonize ourselves we are discovering that there are riches in our own heritage and learning to appreciate them" (1988:20).

B. Tlhagale emphasises that:

> The values and meaning embedded in the African symbol system continue to dominate the African world-view much more radically than meets the eye... The public emergence of African forms of being must challenge the distortion of apartheid Christianity and advocate the rediscovery of the values embedded in the different secular and religious traditions [1985:36].

Clearly Black Theology comes close to African Theology at this point. The relationship between the two is by no means clear and different authors relate them in a spectrum going from inclusion: Black Theology as part of African Theology (Tutu 1978:369), to exclusion: Black Theology is a liberation theology which is intelligeable only in terms of the particularity of the black struggle (Mosala 1986:85).

2.2.4.4 The Theological Context.

Black Theology works within three different theological contexts or keys. It is at different times, a Critical Theology, a Liberation Theology and a Positive Theology.

2.2.4.4.1 Black Theology as a Critical Theology.

As a Critical Theology Black Theology sees its role as one of criticising the prevailing theological understanding in the South African situation which have been used to legitimize the present social situation: the Apartheid State. These theologies it has named collectively "White Theology". Black Theology considers White Theology to be based on Western philosophy, anthropology and thought patterns which it considers to be often foreign both to the Scriptures and to black African understanding[37]

Simon Maimela has produced a scathing indictment of the understanding of man in White Theology as demonstrated by both the current theological position of the white Dutch Reformed Church in South Africa as outlined in its document "Human Relations and the South African scene in the Light of Scripture" as well as in the practice of white Christians in general (Maimela 1981:27-43). According to Maimela, White Theology is permeated with a pessimistic view of man who is fundamentally not good. Man lives under the power of his evil desires and is not to be trusted. Rather, he needs to be controlled, and government is about the social control of humankind which, if left to its own designs will fall prisoner to its own baser instincts and destroy itself. It is an anthropology in which the fundamental attitude is one of suspicion, expecting that which is bad to occur. Man is merely a sinner (1981:31).

----

37. The critical dimension of Black Theology is not confined only to White Theology but also considers all that which has to do with the stewardship of the white man in South Africa and its influence on his consequent apostasy regarding Gospel values. On this point see Buthelezi 1976:198-201.

Black Theology also criticises the Church, especially to the extent that it is tied to Western models of expression and understanding. It contends that the Church is seen as a "white man's Church" and that blacks who join it are seen as moving into the white man's arena. Not only that, but many blacks maintain that the Church has been used as a tool for their subjugation (Cf. de Gruchy 1979:161).

In a certain way, the Church can be considered to be on trial in South Africa. When it becomes a beneficiary of the socio-political structures, as has happened in its history, it then finds it very difficult to challenge the evil within these structures either through reasons of fear, or bacause it becomes blind to them[38]. Clearly this is the situation of some of the white controlled Churches in South Africa. The Apartheid policy itself, for example, has been shown to be essentially the mission policy of the Dutch Reformed Church (Boesak 1984:106).

Allan Boesak sees in Black Theology, an indictment of white Christianity because of what has been done in the name of God in South Africa (1984:56). According to him one of the major fruits of Black Theology is the unmasking of the illusion that Western Christian theology is universal, speaking to all who call themselves Christian. In South Africa, this universal theology has in fact become a White Theology reflecting only the beliefs and understandings of the rich and powerful. Black Theology, in showing that this Theology does not speak for blacks, has unmasked this universalist illusion and put into relief its 'a priori' anthropological, philosophical and cultural presuppositions (1984:55&58).

2.2.4.4.2 Black theology as Liberation Theology.

Probably the most important key that Black Theology works within is the key of Liberation Theology. Indeed many authors have identified this as the fundamental essence of Black Theology. Archbishop Desmond Tutu clearly articulates this position:

> I count Black Theology in the category of liberation theologies....I believe that the Black or liberation theology exponent...is engaged in gut-level issues, in issues of life and death. This sounds melodramatic, but, you see, in the face of an oppressive White racism, it is not a merely academic issue for my Black people when they ask "God, on whose side are you ?" "God are you Black

---

38. The comments of Napoleon are interesting in this regard. Cf. Maimela 1981:19-20.

or White?" "Is it possible to be Black and Christian at the same time?" These are urgent questions and I must apply whatever theological sensitivity and ability I have trying to provide some answers to them under the Gospel...[God] is on the side of the oppressed solely and simply because they are oppressed. Note, however, that he delivers them *from* bondage (all kinds of bondage for us) and delivers them *for* being his people to be his peculiar people. [Tutu 1977:115-116]

Allan Boesak agrees. The Gospel is a Gospel of liberation and therefore Black Theology is a theology of liberation, since God always chooses the side of the weak and down trodden (1984:55).

A Theology of liberation is not just a political ideology or strategy for it deals with the black reality under the light of the word of God (Boesak 1984:56). This word is pre-eminently a message of liberation: "the call to participate with God in the struggle for the Kingdom and justice in the world" (Boesak 1984:58).

Indeed for Boesak, Black Theology offers liberation both to whites as well as to blacks: "telling them that they will never be free from their fear until blacks are free from bondage" (1984:57). Analysing the process of liberation for all, he sees that it entails the total liberation from sin in all its manifestations including economic exploitation, de-humanisation, poverty, suffering, and political oppression. In fact against all that which destroys 'human-being-ness'. "It is a liberation towards a meaningful human existence seeking freedom and human fulfillment. It is liberation for the service of the living God" (1984:74).

2.2.4.4.3 Black Theology as African Theology: Its Positive Mode.

As Black Theology moves into a more positive expression of its vision of man, salvation, and of the Kingdom of God, it finds the need to look for categories of understanding and meaning which reflect the black experience. More and more, Black Theology is turning to African Theology in order to find inspiration.

S. Dwane outlines four theological principles as the framework of this process of inculturation. The first principle results from Creation being "Good". Humanity and human life is basically good. This is expressed in the key African concept of "ubuntu", personhood: "the recognition

and respect of other peoples humanity, and the demands which
their humanity makes upon us as fellow human beings" (Dwane
1988:22).

The second principle is related to the Incarnation
which implies an affirmation of humanity and in this case
the humanity of Africa. In the Incarnation, "God in Christ
tells us that we need not be ashamed of ourselves, our
blackness, our modes of thinking, our norms and values and
our traditional culture because we are the work of his
hands" (1988:22).

The third principle derives from the Easter event of
the death and resurrection and implies that within the
process there will be a sorting of wheat from chaff in the
appropriation of African culture into faith: "God can sort
out African culture just as he has sorted so many others"
(1988:22). The result will be a manifestation of the
glorification of God in man fully alive.

The final principle derives from the Pentecost event
which is an affirmation of the value of all cultures and
their sharing in the common life of the body. It implies a
unity in diversity. Meanings and concepts such as
personhood, life, symbolism, community, relatedness,
fellowship and liminality which derive from African culture,
would play a part here helping in the process of
Inculturation. This area is dealt with in more detail under
African Theology (infra 2.3).

2.2.5 The Theological Content of Black Theology in South Africa.

Mogketi Motlhabi severely reprimands Black Theology in
South Africa as a "non starter" (1986b:38). He contends that
Black Theologians have been too content to rely on American
models and are too caught up in the situation to wish to
reflect on it and analyse it in order to draw up a coherent
system of Black Theology. This is particularly so with
regard to its content. He suggests that the theology has not
yet moved from its "oral" form and can only really be found
in the preaching and pastoral duties of its exponents
(1986b:40).

The judgment is perhaps a little severe and has been
criticised as Motlhabi himself points out (1986b:55n3). Our
own investigation has revealed that the discipline has
already identified several major themes which form the
content of Black Theology. In the literature we have
surveyed, seven themes emerge as the major content of Black
Theology. They can be summarised as follows:

    1. Sin.

2. Salvation.
3. The Black Messiah/ Black God.
4. Black Theology and the Scriptures.
5. Conversion.
6. Faith and Morality.
7. The Black Church.

2.2.5.1 Sin in Black Theology.

Maimela clearly distinguishes between the understanding
of sin in Black Theology and White Theology. White Theology,
in its attempt to be universal, has defined what sin is for
all people and thus for black people. This definition is
legalistic in character understanding sin as transgression
of law (1988:23). He maintains that this definition should
not be accepted by Black Theologians. In the Scripture, he
finds that sin is expressed in terms of the break down in
relationship between God and human beings as well as between
human beings themselves. Sin then refers to a break down in
relatedness and this links to the African concept of
relatedness expressed in phrases such as "umuntu ungumuntu
ngabantu" (a person is a person through and by other people)
a proverb which exists throughout Africa in many languages
(1988:22; Cf. Motlhabi 1986a:94).
   In Black Theology the primary category of sin as a
destruction of relatedness is oppression. It is the primary
category because it is the most urgent one and also because
it is the one the Christian community has been the least
concerned about (Maimela 1986:108). Oppression occurs when
the social system within which people live is opposed to
their realisation as human beings and thus becomes a weight
which crushes them as they attempt to live their lives,
instead of being a means for their upliftment and the
promotion of their humanity (Maimela 1988:17).
   Allan Boesak identifies the process of the systematic
stripping of black people of their human dignity by whites
in South Africa, reducing them to the role of non-persons
(and calling them non-whites) as sinful. He requires that
Black Theology name it as such (1984:6).
   Finally sin is also understood in terms of the
destruction of life. Boesak points out that physical death
is only one kind of death. It is also death when your
human-being-ness is not recognised (1984:51). Maimela points
out that sins and evil in the African context are concerned
with the human attempt to destroy and diminish the life of
others (1988:21-22).

2.2.5.2 Salvation in Black Theology.

Clearly this theme is linked with the preceding one. In Black Theology salvation is first seen as liberation from oppression. It is the liberation which Yahweh wins for his people: the Exodus event which lies at the centre, and is the sustenance, of the life of Israel (Boesak 1977:18).

Black Theology maintains that one cannot speak of the love of God without speaking of his justice as righteousness-in-action. The same message of salvation understood as liberation is at the centre of the New Testament where it is expressed in Jesus' declaration of his purpose and mission in Luke 4:18-22 (Boesak 1977:20-21). Such liberation is concerned not only with the liberation of individuals but also demands the transformation of society in all its dimensions: social, political and economic, since human relatedness, oppression, and thus sin, penetrate deeply into all of these areas.

> For until the totality of that situation - characterized by human brokenness, alienation and, therefore, lack of social justice, freedom, and personal wholeness - is saved, transformed and liberated, there can be no genuine and tangible salvation for humanity. [Maimela 1986:109]

Salvation thus also implies reconciliation. But it is a reconciliation which comes from a recognition of sinfulness and thus the need for forgiveness, as well as an openness to conversion. It is a reconciliation grounded in the decision to work together for the building up of God's Kingdom in mutual respect and unity and not a "cheap reconciliation" which ignores the past and seeks a future which wishes to retain the status quo. It is a reconciliation which is only possible after the establishment of righteouness (Boesak 1977:93).

African Theology has also helped Black Theology in providing a deeper vision of what the Kingdom of God means as the goal of salvation. Salvation, here, is seen as a wholeness in relations between human beings and God, as well as between human beings themselves (Maimela 1988:19). This is expressed in terms such as 'fellowship' (de Gruchy 1979:157) and 'solidarity' (Goba 1974:29).

Closely linked to this is the concept of salvation understood as "harmony and peace in community life" (Setiloane 1986:82). In the same vein, Boesak speaks of salvation as being fully human. It is the "courage to be" (1977:48-49; Cf. Tillich as cited) and contains a dimension of power: human power, which is grounded in the power of

God. To share in this power is to be fully human. In this way human beings becomes the subjects of their own humanity thus becoming truly human (1977:151).

Clearly this is Salvation as realised eschatology and Black Theology freely admits to this emphasis. It is concerned with an existential situation and the manifestation of the Kingdom of God within it. Black Theology does not deny the future eschatological reality of salvation but it is not at present a priority and indeed presents a sometimes dangerous orientation in that the future eschatological vision of the Kingdom has often mitigated against attempting to establish it in the present human condition. Black Theology is currently concerned with overcoming this tendency (Maimela 1986:107-112).

2.2.5.3 The Black Messiah.

The concept of the Black Messiah is linked to the question of the cultural appropriation of Christ. In Black Theology, however, its primary meaning is linked with the idea of God taking sides. Black people ask themselves if the God whom the white people have acknowledged in their history in South Africa can be the God of blacks who consider themselves the victims of a history which has resulted in the present situation. Already in 1971, Tutu asks the question: "God - Black Or White?" (Tutu 1971:111).

> When disaster has struck the black community - a train crash on the Soweto line, a mine disaster, a bus accident or what have you - then the spoken or unspoken anguished cry is "But why does it always happen to us?" not "Why is there evil or suffering in the universe of a good and loving God?" It is "why do *we* suffer so much?" not, " Why do men suffer?" And the naive answer is "God is not on our side." "The black man is God's step child." [Tutu 1971:113]

Bonganjalo Goba affirms that it is precisely because of their situation that God is on the side of the black people in South Africa. For the God of the Bible is also the God of the poor and oppressed. He is the God who will liberate them from their suffering and call them to the mission of building His Kingdom (1986b:58).

Allan Boesak is the theologian who uses the term "Black Messiah" in the South African context (1977:41). In this he follows American theologians such as James Cone and Albert Cleage[39]. If Jesus is to be the incarnation of God in his

----

39. Cone identifies blackness with oppression and liberation so that every oppressed person on the road to liberation is ipso facto black

40

people, then Boesak affirms that for black Christians, Jesus, understood as the Black Messiah, is "the only true confession for our time" (1977:42).

2.2.5.4 Black Theology and the Scriptures.

Black Theologians in South Africa have two basic positions regarding the Scriptures. A more traditional position is taken by authors such as Boesak and Tutu who see the word of God as the inspiration and light which leads and transforms the black community along its journey. The Word of God is a refusal to believe that the powers of this world have the final say on the situation (Boesak 1984:33). It is to be heard in such a way that it becomes Good News for blacks, illuminating the situation in which they find themselves (1984:xi).

Goba interprets Tutu's understanding of Scripture in a similar way insisting on the "theocentric" interpretation in which God is the main actor. This same God continues to act in human history today in the same way as he did in the Bible (Goba 1986a:65-66).

A second, more radical, view of the role of the Bible is offered principally by I. Mosala (1986:176-199; 1989). Instead of interpreting the situation in the light of the Scriptures, he considers it necessary to interpret the Scriptures in the light of the situation. The starting point is the material condition and situation of black people in South Africa today. This becomes the "epistemological lens" through which the Bible is read (1986:185-187). In this way, not all the Bible is 'Word of God'. For if that were so one would have to accept all of it since God's word cannot be the object of criticism (1986:178). According to Mosala, it is impossible to claim the whole of the Bible in support of Black Theology because the Bible itself contains theological positions and arises out of particular contexts. Following Brueggemann, he suggests that in the Old Testament, two covenant traditions can be detected: a Davidic Tradition and a Mosaic tradition (1986:195). These represent different social, political and ideological tendencies. Mosala's point is that one needs to be aware of the ideological presuppositions present both in the text of Scripture and in the reader before a valid hermeneutic can be done, and that

----

(Boesak 1977:17). Albert Cleage goes even further, attempting to add a historical dimension maintaining that: "Jesus was a black Jew whose purpose was to form a Black Christian Nation which would stand up to white oppression" (Motlhabi 1986b:42-3; Cf. also Boesak 1977:142). Cleage's assertions are not accepted by many other black theologians.

in consequence, some parts of the Scripture will be too far
removed from the ideological, political, social and cultural
situation of blacks to be able to speak to them in a
coherent Black Theology of Liberation (1986:197).

2.2.5.5 Conversion.

The Word of God evokes a response from people as it
speaks to them in and of their situation. This response is a
turning towards God and his will and, consequently, away
from sin and evil. It is the process called conversion: a
theme which has been dealt with by some South African Black
Theologians. Maimela points out that it is conversion which
overcomes human conflicts and leads to the move from
oppressive and exploitative tendencies towards solidarity
between the oppressed and the oppressor (Maimela
1986:104-105). It involves an acknowledgment of sin, a
request for forgiveness and a willingness to forgo anger and
retribution (Cf. Buthelezi 1976b).

Allan Boesak points out that we have to look beyond
the limits of the present situation to discover the
possibilities of reconciliation and genuine community. This
is metanoia and grace, and it does not come cheap. It
demands a conversion for "blacks to be reconciled with
themselves as well as for whites to also be reconciled with
themselves and to accept blackness as authentic humanity"
(1977:30). Only in this way can both begin to live more
truly human lives.

Maimela in another article, understands conversion as
the linking together of right believing and right doing.
Conversion comes when faith begins to live. In a South
Africa which considers itself a Christian country, such a
testing of faith by the behaviour of Christians has now
become essential (Maimela 1988:24-25).

2.2.5.6 Faith and Morality.

As we have just seen, Maimela links faith with right
living and doing. The ethical dimension of faith has a
priority in Black Theology. Makhatini describes faith as day
to day living. Black Theology has the responsibility to
awaken blacks to their calling to make their faith effective
from day to day. Unfortunately, Christianity has often been
presented as a two hour Sunday concern. This is contrary to
the black man's cultural understanding of religion as
permeating the whole of life (Makhatini 1973:15).

Boesak sees Black Theology as the quintessential expression of the faith of black Christians (1984:10) and the "only authentic way for blacks to pursue their Christian faith" (1984:56). Some authors understand this faith in terms of an empowerment which a person receives from God in order that he might find the strength to be the one whom God has called him to be. Thus Kunnie directly links faith with empowerment defining it as:

> The component of human experience in relation to the transcendent which vivifies the body of religion..... This faith is not a superficial relationship, it is the medium by which the believer becomes personally and collectively empowered. [1986:163-164)

He takes issue with the Black Liberation Theologians for having neglected the essentially religious dimension of psychic liberation (1986:156).

2.2.5.7 The Black Church.

The concept of the Black Church is not well defined but crops up in the writings of many authors[40]. These authors do not agree on what exactly is meant by the term "Black Church". Sometimes the term is used in a sociological sense, meaning the group of black Christians without any necessary ontological character manifest in structures or organisations. It rather seems to refer to a movement expressed within the existing Churches. Ntwasa's early definition was exclusive and very restrictive in terms of its condition for entry both regarding race and level of commitment: "The Church is that company of people who 'die with Christ' in the quality of life which is totally committed to liberating black people" (1973:115). Boesak attempts to follow the same kind of line whilst broadening the base in his definition. For him, the Church is "A broad movement of black Christians joined in black solidarity that transcends all barriers of denomination and ethnicity" (1984:21).

For Simon Maimela, to speak of the black Church means to speak of all the Churches in South Africa except for the white Dutch Reformed Church since these Churches are all at least 80% black in membership (1988:16). Goba starts out with a theological understanding of Church as "laos, the people of God, called into being by Jesus Christ to

---

40. Boesak 1984:20-31; Maimela 1988:15-25; Goba 1982:26-33; Lamola 1988:5-15; Ngcokovane 1988 26-34; Ntwasa 1974:109-118; Cf. also terms such as "Black Christian Community" Goba 1986b:58

participate in the liberating activity of God in the World"
(1982:27). Within this definition he adopts a sociological
understanding of the black urban Church as those Churches
which have black African membership and an African ethos
(1982:28-29).

All these authors are Protestant and present an
ecclesiology which seems to understand the Church
manifesting its unity on a transcendental level whilst being
pluriform in its actual expression within the people of God.
In this way, the Church seems to be understood as a grouping
of institutions rather than a single institution as Goba
would have us believe. It is the fact that these
institutions are either totally or overwhelmingly black
which renders them a Black Church[41].

Lamola takes a different position. He considers that
the Black Church is not yet realised. When it is, it will be
an "African Church independent of the White Man" (1988:5).
He posits the African Independent Churches as model for such
a Church but maintains that until a contextual Systematic
Theology has been constructed, the Black Church will remain
unrealised (1988:6).

2.2.6 The Method of Black Theology.

As with other Contextual Theologies, the methodology of
Black Theology takes the context as its starting point. In
this case it is the concrete situation of the black man. It
then attempts to mediate and understand the Gospel in
relationship to this base experience (Buthelezi 1973:23-24).
Indeed, as Mofokeng points out, the theology came into
existence because of the problem which blacks faced: the
inability of traditional theology to express and reflect the
black experience of the Gospel as well as the tendency of
traditional theology to work against black people and their
aspirations (Mofokeng 1986:122-123).

To the extent that Black Theology is a theology of
Liberation, the focus of the methodology is the "struggle":
the progressive process of confronting social evil and
working for social change. There is little agreement
regarding the way in which this process should be carried
out, but it is the function of Black Theology to reflect on

---

41. Whites seem to be members of the Black Church either as a minority
(Maimela) or by virtue of having "taken on a condition of blackness by
participating in the struggle for liberation" (Boesak 1984:22)! This
clearly contradicts Goba's understanding as outlined in the section on
the racial context of Black Theology (2.2.4.2). Whites are specifically
excluded in Ntwasa's original definition (1974:117).

this process in an attempt to discover God's will and presence within it, as well as the power from him to continue with it.

Authors such as Allan Boesak and Desmond Tutu reflect a more traditional approach, allowing the Gospel and the faith of Christians to make Christ present in the midst of the struggle (Boesak 1984:74-78; 1977:15-16). Others, such as Mofokeng and Mosala search for greater clarity in the understanding of the structure and workings of this process. Both of them opt for a Historical Materialist approach in which a Marxian social Analysis is applied to the current situation and a comparison is made with a similar analysis of Scriptural situations and the praxis of Jesus (Mofokeng 1986:125; Mosala 1986:185-197).

Clearly ideological factors are present here as well as polemics, which could perhaps be eliminated by a better understanding of the language used. There is agreement that Black Theology is seen as an ascending theology having its starting point in life which it tries to render intelligible in terms of faith and the Scriptures. Nevertheless much work remains to be done in order to construct a comprehensive and mutually intelligible methodology. Motlhabi is optimistic that this can be achieved.

> It is tempting to interpret the South Africa views of Black Theology....as almost contradictory and perhaps representing irreconcilable schools of thought. However, one should understand them more as formative stages in determining the method of Black Theology which may ultimately be reconciled as issues and interconnections become clearer and Black Theology itself matures. [Motlhabi 1986b:48]

2.2.7 Reflection on the Phenomenon.

The phenomenon of Black Theology has had a major impact on the Church in South Africa. This impact has perhaps been greater than its proponents realise. In a certain way, it is providing a creative thrust which is having an effect within the whole Church. We have, for example, already noted its contribution to the birth of Prophetic Theology (supra 2.1.2). Black Theology's value lies within its frame of reference as a Contextual Theology: part of the total process of reflection of the Church as a whole. Sometimes, however, its authors are guilty of absolutising the experience, the reflection and the method of Black Theology. They do this when they identity all oppressed as black or when they speak of a black Church or of only a part of the Scripture being God's Word. Within the theological framework of Black Theology and its language, used as a technical theological language, these assertions may well be true. But they are easily taken out of context and one does sometimes get the impression that preconceived ideologies are speaking rather than a reflection on the real lived experience of black people.

One of the major difficulties this author has, is with the affirmation of some Black Theologians that one group of people, the blacks, can be equated with the People of God: the Church. It seems to result from the tendency to absolutise the context and consequently, these theologians seem to run the risk of falling into the same error that it has accused White or Western theology of making. David Bosch has posed the following question:

> We have to ask in all seriousness whether the category 'people' or 'nation' may be the object of the church's concern for liberation. 'People' as a cultural and ethnic entity is *not* a theological category and whenever it is made into such a category....it cannot but lead to mutual exclusiveness which endangers the life of the Church as the new community. [Bosch 1977:334]

Bosch speaks from within the Afrikaner community which has had the experience of falsely arrogating to itself the term "People of God" specially chosen by Him in a particular situation[42].

The comments of Bosch have been attacked both by Afrikaner Theologians and Black Theologians (de Gruchy 1979:167) but it is surely necessary to expose the danger of absolutising ones experience without negating the value of a theology in its context. The problem occurs when language which is true and valid within its context is translated outside the context. When this happens, its veracity can no longer be guaranteed and a new process of reflection is required.

The dearth of Catholic Theologians participating in the Black Theology debate is unfortunate. An ontological ecclesiology for Black Theology is clearly needed and would help to situate the debate more clearly within the totality of the People of God.

----

42. "Apartheid is based on what the Afrikaner believes to be his divine calling and his privilege - to convert the heathen to Christianity without obliterating his National identity" D.F. Malan, "Apartheid: South Africa's answer to a major problem" , Pretoria, State Information Office, 1954. quoted in Mermelstein 1987:95.

2.3 AFRICAN THEOLOGY.

2.3.1 Introduction.

African Theology emerged in Sub-Saharan Africa during the 1960's and 1970's as an attempt to "root the Gospel in a culture" (Dwane 1988:20), to explore the relationship between the Gospel and African culture (Mbiti 1977:26) and to "reflect upon and express the Christian faith in African thought patterns" (Muzorewa 1985:95).

It is not our purpose to explore African Theology as such in this paper. We are more concerned with the fact that African Theology has begun to emerge as an important discipline in the South African ecclesial situation and is therefore one of the phenomena which we wish to examine. In South Africa, African Theology has had a different genesis in that it is becoming important only subsequent to Black Theology and is emerging as Black Theologians have begun to become aware of the need to look at African culture as a mode of expression, thought and reflection (Mogoba 1985:14). This has meant that African Theology in South Africa has both commonalities and differences with that of Central Africa. Our purpose here is to observe how African Theology is being received, understood, and developed in the South African situation.

2.3.2 The Relationship between Black Theology and African Theology in South Africa.

There is no consensus on this relationship in South Africa and it seems that very often the problem is one of language. Different authors give different contents to the terms "African Theology" and "Black Theology" and then compare these on the basis of the content ascribed. Clearly the relationship between the two is dependent on this content. Many authors see African Theology in terms of the relationship between African culture on the one hand and faith or the Gospel on the other. This is contrasted to Black Theology which is seen as having more to do with the social situation, its immorality, and a praxis for changing it. Thus for Goba, Black Theology and African Theology need to be distinguished, since African Theology has an ethnographical or cultural hermeneutic whereas Black Theology has a political one (Goba 1986b:61). Clearly African theologians such as Jean-Marc Ela would not fit simply into Goba's categories (Cf. Ela 1986).

Other authors, such as Desmond Tutu, maintain that Black Theology is part of African Theology and brings an important dimension to it (Tutu 1975). He believes that African Theology has been valuable by "addressing the split in the African soul" but that it has failed in relating faith to the modern problematic of life in Africa today. It is here that Black Theology makes it contribution to African Theology (1978:369). Mokgethi Motlhabi also questions the traditional distinction of Black Theology as a Contextual Theology and African Theology as an Indigenous Theology as if contextualization and indigenization were incompatible (1986b:40). Simon Maimela echoes the same opinion. Writing on the question of the identity of the Black Church, he suggests that "The African perspective on life is the heritage that Black Christians should bring to the Church" (1988:22). Consequently Black Theology in South Africa would become inauthentic if it were not African in nature.

2.3.3 Towards a Definition of African Theology.

African Theology is usually defined by South African authors in terms of two categories. The first category is predominantly cultural, ideological and intellectual in nature. African Theology here is the attempt to express the Christian faith in terms of African patterns of understanding[43].

The South African theologians wish to introduce an existential category to African Theology. As we have already noted, this dimension is linked with the situation within which African Christians are living now. It especially emphasises the social and economic dimension and has its source in Black Theology. Already in 1971 Desmond Tutu was criticising Western Theology as being over occupied with providing answers to intellectual questions which were already answered in the African mind. He writes: "The crisis of faith for the African is not basically intellectual. It is much more deeply existential" (1971:112-113). The question of evil, for example, is experienced as an existential rather than an intellectual problem. "The black

----

43. Muzorewa's collection of definition by different authors expresses this mode of understanding (1985:95-97). African Theology: "...seeks to reflect upon and express the Christian faith in African thought forms and idiom..." (Kurewa); "...is expressed in categories of thought which arise out of the philosophy of African peoples..." (All Africa Council of Churches definition); "...is theological reflection and expression by African Christians" (Mbiti). These definitions reflect Mbiti's understanding that Gospel, culture and faith together produce Christianity (1977:26f).

man believes that he labours under some divine or satanic curse to suffer, to fail, to bungle and then to suffer yet again. This I contend is the heart of the crisis in our faith" (1971:113).

African Theology, according to Tutu, needs to respond to the quest of the African to live an authentic Christian Life in the face of an existential reality which seems to deny God's presence or his concern. A situation in which the white man always seems to come out on top. For this reason, the central questions are: "But on whose side is God?" and "Why do we suffer so much?" Consequently he asks for an African Theology to be concerned for the poor and the oppressed, about man's need for liberation from all kinds of bondage" (1971:113).

2.3.4 The Content of African Theology in the South African Situation: Major Themes.

2.3.4.1 Towards a New Understanding of Culture and Intercultural Communication.

Discussions regarding the content and understanding of the term "African Culture" provokes much controversy in the South African Context. There are several reasons for this. Firstly, the term 'culture' has been used within the Apartheid ideology to justify some of the governments racial policies. As a result, it is viewed with a suspicion which is not found elsewhere. Secondly, South Africa is the most industrialised and urbanised country on the continent and many blacks living in the urban areas have been through, or are going through, cultural destruction and mutation as part of an acculturation process. Because of this, categories and patterns of understanding found in Traditional African Culture do not apply in the same way today as they did in the past. Thirdly, South Africa is an extremely culturally diverse country in which not all black people share a common Traditional African cultural heritage. Various Asian and European cultural traditions are the roots, together with Traditional African Culture, of the cultural heritage of those people who today refer to themselves as black. Finally, the country has five million white people who are also diverse, both in their own cultural traditions and in their present cultural expressions. It is relatively clear that communication and understanding between these groups is important if they are to live in the same country. However, up to now, the model of transcultural communication has been the imposition of the will of one cultural group upon all the others: a unilinear model. African Theology contends that this should not be the case in a future South Africa.

For Tlhagale, the fundamental question here is: "Can culture be cast into a creative mold that will transcend the symbols of conflict and yet retain ethnic histories and events that give meaning and direction to the diverse population groups of South Africa" (Tlhagale 1985:33)?

He answers that this will not happen if culture is perceived only in terms of social heritage or in terms of an ideology which maintains the interests of the dominant class. This, he maintains is the understanding of culture that the South African Government currently propagates (1985:29-30). Nor does he believe that a model of open cultural pluralism expressed as federalism would work in the South African Society. For he claims that this does not deal with the socio-economic fact of class division in South Africa[44].

Tlhagale sees the ideal as the emergence of a new, fully African, culture in South Africa. This implies the development of a fund of common meaning with which all groups can identify. The development of a common meaning implies the willingness to engage in mutual dialogue to search for "clarification, mutual understanding and eventual transcendence of meanings embedded in the diverse racial groupings"(1983:117). Clearly such a search will mean sacrifice on the part of all groups and not just on the part of the weaker as in the past.

2.3.4.2 Enduring Aspects of Traditional African Culture.

Mogoba and Setiloane have both indicated the extent to which an African world view and cultural meanings continue to persist amongst African peoples who have been exposed to Western influence for a long period of time. This perseverance is often much more than is readily visible at first glance and so is a deeper phenomenon than would seem at first sight[45].

Mogoba stresses the importance of getting to the roots of the fact "that inside their own bosoms there is something which they cannot explain; something which draws them together with their forebears - call them ancestors if you wish" (1985:8). It is part of the task of African Theology and African cultural research to understand, integrate and

----

44. "The content of transracial communication can therefore not confine itself to the question of racial harmony, but must also address itself to the fundamental contradiction that expresses itself in material and political terms. Both the economic system and the power structure must be brought into question" (Tlhagale 1983:120; Cf. also 1985:34).

45. Mogoba 1985:7-8; Setiloane 1978:402; Cf. also Tlhagale 1985:36.

express these modes of being as a condition for the possibility of dialogue. Gabriel Setiloane is the author who has perhaps done most to probe, interpret and express this world view in theological categories. Some of the major concepts he has written about are:

-An African Cosmogony (1975:29-31).

-The fundamental concept of "Ubuntu" (personhood) (1975:31; 1978:408).

-The concept of relatedness-in-community as the fundamental mode of human existence (1975:31).

-The role of the Divine as underpinning African community (1975:32&35).

-A world view which includes the visible and the numinous as one reality and thus sees death (to this world) neither as an end of life nor as a moving away from humanity or the world (1978:403).

These concepts have important consequences for cultural understanding. Ancestors are important for they are still present and active in the world (1978:406). The concept of salvation is understood as the fullness (wholeness) of humanity (1986:82). Finally, the understanding of the land is central, for it is the place where the community is rooted through the enduring presence of members who have gone before (1978:410).

2.3.4.3 Salvation.

This theme has already been dealt with under Black Theology. There it was noted that it is African Theology which provides the vision of the Kingdom of God and Salvation from the African Cultural point of view (supra 2.2.5.2). The South African authors highlight three aspects: Salvation as wholeness; Salvation as life and Salvation as relatedness.

Salvation as wholeness concerns the harmonious functioning and manifestation of being. It is being, being what it should be. Setiloane refers to salvation in this mode as: "A situation in which harmony and peace prevail in community life" (1986:82). The "situation" and "life" referred to is the African understanding of life: both that which is seen by the eyes and that which is there but numinous (1986:72).

Closely linked to this is the vision of salvation as life. Buthelezi has pointed out that the major characteristic of African Traditional Religion was wholeness of life and that thus religion and life belonged together. Indeed "religion was life" (1974:99). By the same token, then, Christianity is life and God is seen as the source of this life (Mogoba 1985:9). Here life is recognised as a force which is not specified but somehow conceived in terms of a presence, which being of God, is a sacred presence. "All being is charged with this sacredness because of being so penetrated and permeated by "Modimo" (Southern Sotho term for God)"[46]. This life presence of God is the "force or energy within which relationships between man and man and group and group are enacted" (Setiloane 1975:33).

This last quotation brings us to the understanding of salvation in terms of relatedness. For African Theology, salvation as the event of an individual soul, is foreign. This is because persons are fundamentally related. Salvation in this mode refers to the manifestation of harmonious and peaceful relationships between persons and groups. This clearly has important consequences for morality, and to the extent that persons and groups live in wholeness of life in their relationships, then salvation and indeed, as we shall see later, health, are manifested. And to the extent that these relationships are not whole, then the group is sick and salvation is not present: "For life is a totality and salvation is when it is kept so" (Setiloane 1986:78).

2.3.4.4 Christology.

This is one of the most vital areas of present day research in African Theology and one in which the South African authors consider that they have an important contribution to make.

Setiloane sees Christ as the one in whom Divinity, in its African sense of force and power, has been most fully manifest. In this sense, Jesus Christ is Lord. He is Lord because of his incarnation, death and resurrection at a point in time during the past. But he is also Lord as a living presence through the dynamic presence of the Divinity manifest in the life of people here and now (1975:35). This emphasis has led to African Theologians being accused of presenting a theology of Christ which Daneel describes as emphasising a "theologiae gloriae" at the expense of a

----

46. Setiloane 1975:33. Note also that the concept of "Modimo" as God does not fully correspond with the Western concept as the author explains in the article.

"theologiae Crucis" (1984:78-79). Chikane maintains that the South African Theologians have helped to redress this balance through the contribution, from Black Theology, to the theology of suffering, in which the suffering of black people is related to the experience of Christ on the cross. "The experience of suffering in the black community makes sense when we believe that Jesus suffered... Jesus liberates us precisely by this suffering." (1985:42).

Buthelezi, after drawing the normal distinction between oppressive and redemptive suffering, asserts that the suffering of black people in South Africa is becoming redemptive rather than oppressive. The reason for this is that blacks are seeing their suffering as a step towards liberation rather than a cry of self pity (1976:180). In this way, the crisis of faith about which Tutu spoke some years earlier is being resolved (1971:113-116; supra 2.2.4.4.2).

Finally, many authors have suggested that the starting point for an African Christology should be Christ the Healer[47]. The phenomenon of healing and the link with Christ's role as healer is so important in South Africa today that it is considered a separate phenomenon and will be treated later (infra 3.1).

2.3.4.5 Morality.

We have already noted that the idea of morality in African Theology is intimately linked with that of salvation since the concept of "life" is at the root of both of them (supra 2.3.4.3). Motlhabi cites Häring's platitude that morality is for persons and goes on to note that in African Culture the root value of personhood is "Ubuntu" already referred to earlier (1986a:94&97; supra 2.3.4.2). This term is difficult to translate into Western languages without reducing its content. Consequently it has the possibility of providing African Theology with the means of making a significant contribution to theology in general. The term refers to a wholeness or fullness of personhood or humanness as a communicable value in human relations. The promotion of "Ubuntu" implies a morality directed to harmonious relations between people implying values such as honesty, compassion, truthfulness and kindness (Cf. Magoba 1985:9; Motlhabi 1986a:94). Such relationships are based on the value of respect, another root value of morality in African Culture and Theology[48] .

----
47. Cf. Daneel 1984:84; Setiloane 1979:64.

48. Class Notes, Boka di Mpasi, Londi 1989.

Since the family is the principal arena of moral education and formation, it is clear that Christian morality passed on from one generation to another is permeated with the lived expression of faith in the culture of the people concerned. Such formation is thus an already lived African Theology and perhaps one of the most important areas for future investigation (Cf. Mbiti 1977:31).

2.3.4.6 Modes of Worship.

Perhaps more work has been done in this area than any other. The liturgy in Africa has been a relatively safe and easy area in which to "indigenise" the faith and much progress has been made since the "Missa Luba" of the early 1960's. South African progress in this area has lagged the rest of the continent although some steps have been taken especially through the Lumko Missiological Institute[49]. Since Worship is an expression of faith, it is clear that such expression should be coherent with the culture of the people whose faith it expresses (Cf. Mbiti 1977:31). Nevertheless, the identification of African Cultural religious forms as pagan during the acculturation phase between Western Christianity and African Traditional Culture during the missionary period, has left a legacy of confusion and suspicion in the mind of both African Christians and the wider Ecclesial community.

Mbiti calls for greater study and analysis of African culture in order that a more relevant spirituality and mode of worship may emerge (1977:31). Mogoba suggests that African expressions of worship can bring a new appreciation of the importance and role of symbols to the whole Church. He suggests that symbols open the road to the ineffable and that African Christianity already supplies a richness of symbolism (Mogoba 1985:9). Dwane offers two examples in which the symbols of African Traditional custom have been adapted and incorporated into Christian Expression:

> In South Africa, amongst Xhosa people, the custom observed at child birth as a way of introducing the newly-born to its living family and ancestry is

----

49. The Lumko Missiological Institute was founded with the aim of helping the Church, especially in Africa, to develop programmes aimed at the training and formation of lay leaders within the community. It has an extensive series of publications on themes such as: training lay ministers, Small Christian Communities and training for community ministries. The music department is involved with developing indigenous musical forms in the liturgy and has produced a series of cassette tapes and booklets. It also runs music workshops throughout South Africa. The Institute is currently based in Germiston, South Africa.

54

sometimes associated with the baptism of the infant. The other is the "ukubuyisa" festival by which the deceased head of the family is formally and ritually declared an ancestral spirit. Some Christian families will now observe this ritual at the time of the unveiling of the tombstone, a form of service recognised by the Church. [Dwane 1988:24-25]

There is much work still to be done in this area and South Africa has much to learn from the experience of the rest of the continent on the issues of worship, liturgy and spirituality in an African key.

2.3.4.7 The Importance of Liminality.

Closely related with the previous section is the understanding of liminality which plays an important part in African ritual (Ngubane 1986:76). Witbooi outlines the major transition processes for the now extinct Khoikhoi people of South Africa as childbirth, marriage, puberty, bereavement rites, and reception into the rank of hunters. The purpose of these rites was to re-establish the harmony upset by the change brought about by the transition. The rite also helped to establish the new status within the community of a person crossing a threshold (1986:102).

Both Witbooi and Mogoba allude to the fact that many of these rites are still practiced by Christians but that the practice is confused as it is often done in secret for fear of Church leaders. This, too, is an area requiring study in order to discover in what way a contribution may be brought to African Theology (Witbooi 1986h:108; Mogoba 1985:12). The link between liminality rituals and the re-establishment of harmony again indicates the centrality of this latter category in the African cultural framework.

2.3.5. Problems in African Theology.

We have indicated some of the important themes and trends in African Theology as it revealing itself in South Africa today. We wish to close this section by outlining two of the major problems which African Theology must face according to the South African authors if it is to bring a valid contribution to theology in general.

The first concerns the issue of the general and the particular as it applies to African culture and theology. Mogoba has pointed out that African Theology has often been accused of generalising the experiences of one or other tribe into a general African cultural experience; or of generalising the faith of one group of people as a general African experience of faith upon which one can construct an African Theology. Such generalisations are to be avoided since both similarities and differences exist amongst the various groups. He points out, for example, that the role of ancestors does not seem to be so important for tribes such as the Masai, Bushmen or Hottentots whereas for other groups, this is an important African cultural phenomenon (1985:12-13). Although Mogoba does not mention it, studies in Social Anthropology indicate that one would expect cultural differences between hunter/gatherer peoples and more pastorally oriented groups. So whilst Mogoba's caveat needs to be taken seriously, perhaps the differences between the various groups are not as great as he would have us imagine. Nevertheless his adjoinder to go into particular areas and to carry out studies to see what is happening in order to test theories would seem to be a wise one.

Such a practice would also seem important in order to respond to another difficulty which some authors see in African Theology. This is the tendency to look back at pre-colonial African Tradition as the model for African culture today. Many South African authors have spoken out against this, noting that culture is a lived, dynamic reality which changes and adapts to the situation[50]. Buthelezi refers to the tendency to highlight the romantic elements of the African cultural past which is very often a projection by missionaries, appalled by the secularization in their home countries, of the need to return to a more sacral expression of religion (1973:21). A more important criticism is made by Tlhagale whose analysis of African culture today in South Africa is an eloquent plea for an African Theology linked with the socio-economic and political realities of modern African culture, especially in South Africa, as well as a rediscovery of the values, symbols, and cultural heritage which have persevered through to today.

> The public emergence of African forms of being must challenge the distortions of apartheid Christianity and advocate the rediscovery of value embedded in the different secular and religious traditions. This is the daunting task which lies ahead for those who have faith in Africa and are equally committed to seeing persons become cultural beings. [Tlhagale 1985:36]

----
50. Cf. Magoba 1985:13; Tutu 1978:368; Buthelezi 1973:20-21; Tlhagale 1985: 35-36.

CHAPTER THREE

TWO EMERGING PASTORAL RESPONSES

3.1. THE GROWTH OF THE COPING/HEALING CHURCHES.

3.1.1 Introduction.

Between the years 1970 and 1990, one of the most visible phenomena in South African Christianity has been the growth of the independent, nondenominational Churches. A large number of Churches have emerged, calling people to a form of Christianity which stresses the positive, felt experience of the presence of God in a persons life. The growth of these Churches testifies to the existence of a felt need to which this form of Christianity seems to be responding (Morran & Schlemmer 1984:1).

This phenomenon is by no means unique to South Africa and David Barrett has pointed out that this type of Christianity has been growing rapidly throughout the world since the beginning of this century. In 1900 they formed 0.7% of all Christians. This figure had risen to 6% by 1970, 20% by 1988, and is estimated to become 26% of all Christians by the year 2000 (Barrett 1988:18).

However, the uniqueness of the South African situation lies in the fact that this group, collectively, is already the largest Christian grouping in the country, representing about 30% of all Christians and 50% of Black African Christians[51].

In the South African context, these Churches are easily divisible into two main groupings. The first is the African Independent Churches which attempt to express faith in terms of African Cultural patterns. The second grouping are the predominantly white Pentecostal and neo-Pentecostal Churches which are attempting to respond to prevalent Western cultural patterns.

Despite this division, both groups have much in common. They can both trace some of their roots to the Pentecostal, Revival, and Holiness movements prevalent in the United States during the latter part of the nineteenth century and the earlier part of this century (Morran & Schlemmer 1984:2). They also have a similarity of emphasis, laying a

---

51. Cf. Scholten 1983:236-240 on an analysis of the religious affiliation of South Africans according to the 1980 census.

predominant stress on healing, the presence of the Spirit acting amongst them, Scriptural fundamentalism, and on the access to religious experience through the emotions.

One does not want to negate at the outset the fact that the Spirit continues to act in the world. Indeed we will try to show that all of the phenomena which we are considering are signs of His presence in our time. However we contend that much of the appeal of these Churches and movements is due to the fact that they provide a means for people to deal with the pressures and stresses of the life they have to live. They are Churches which help people to cope, and the healing that they provide is precisely the ability to find a coherent life style in a hostile world. It is for this reason that we refer to this phenomenon as "The Growth of the Coping/Healing Churches". The religious dimension of this fact is not denied: clearly the Holy Spirit is also the Paraclete (Jn. 14,16-17). Indeed we shall assert that they provide an important indication of the direction in which the Holy Spirit is calling the whole ecclesial community.

3.1.2 The African Independent Churches.

In 1980, nineteen million people, 76% of the South African population, referred to themselves as Christians. Of these, more than five million people, or almost 30% of Christians in South Africa, are members of the African Independent Churches. This group is thus the largest Christian grouping in the country (Scholten 1983:237).

These figures give a sense of the explosion in the popularity of these Churches amongst the black population of the country. It has been estimated that there are as many as five thousand of these Churches with membership ranging from as few as ten to Churches such as the Zion Christian Church of Bishop Lekhanyane which has more than three quarters of a million members (Scholten 1983:237).

These Churches have developed a synthesis between Christianity and traditional African values and Cultural Practice (Villa-Vicencio 1988:35). In urban areas, in particular, they have become a substitute for the extended family, community, and the sacral practice which formed part of traditional life in the rural areas (Kiernan 1981:142).

3.1.2.1 Healing in Traditional Zulu Culture.

In order to understand the phenomenon of healing in the African Independent Churches, it is necessary to attempt to understand its meaning in traditional African culture. Here

we refer to the Zulu culture which is relatively typical.
There are sicknesses which manifest themselves in a person
as a result of the upsetting of the natural harmony of the
person in his environment. These are called "izifo zabantu"
(sicknesses of the people) and are different to bodily
sickness which can be cured by natural medicines[52]. It is
important to understand that a person can never be
understood in isolation from his environment. When a person
is alive and well it is said that he has life "unempilo"[53].
The opposite to sickness in the Zulu language is life and
when a person is well, or as we would say in English, is
"healthy", then in Zulu, he is said to have life "unempilo".
Sickness is seen as a removal of life and that is why the
sickness of the people is called "ukufa kwabantu" (lit.
"people's death"). Healing is fundamentally, then, the
restoration of life. 'Life' is also understood in terms of
the relatedness between people in community and sickness is
consequently also understood in terms of the disturbance of
the harmony in human relations[54].

----

52. Harriet Ngubane (1977:22-23) explains sickness in Zulu culture in
terms of the following categories:

"Isifo" (English closest equivalent: sickness)
    This is a generic term which refers to all forms of sickness. It
    refers not only to illness but also to various forms of misfortune
    as well as the disposition of being vulnerable to misfortune and
    disease.

"Izifo" (Plural of "Isifo"). These can be of two kinds:
    (a). "Umkuhlane".
    This is a bodily sickness which is due to the ordinary breakdown
    of the body and is not attributable to external forces. It is
    cured by natural medicines (imithi) which are effective in
    themselves and whose use is not ritualized .
    Western medicines and procedures are accepted by Zulus and usually
    understood as fitting into this kind of healing process.

    (b)."Izifo zabantu" or "Ukufa kwabantu" Lit. "sicknesses of the
    people" or "death of the people"

53. "umuntu onempilo" (lit. a person who has life) is one who is
naturally in harmony with his world. That world: what one could refer to
in English as "environment", comprises principally his family, his clan
and his "amadlozi" (nearest English: "ancestors"). Environment is
however not the right word as it connotates what is around the person
and thus external to him. In the Zulu weltenschauung this "environment"
is part of him and constituent of him. It is part of what goes to make
up who he is (McGreal 1988:12).

54. Umuntu: a person, is always man as being-in-community. The Zulus
say "umuntu ungumuntu ngabantu" ("a person is a person through other
people"). Setiloane expresses person as a dynamic concept understanding
the human person as if it were a magnet creating with other persons a
complex [magnetic] field (1975:31). Consequently any disturbance or
imbalance within this universe of his being will have an impact on him

3.1.2.2 Healing in the African Independent Churches.

A clear manifestation of healing as the restoration of
life and harmony is found in the African Independent
Churches. Daneel refers to these as "healing institutions"
in which "their diagnostic and therapeutic work are based
largely on the insights and practices of the *nganga*
[traditional healer]" (Daneel 1983a:86-87). These Churches
tend to operate within the world view of traditional African
Religion and Culture which is interpreted and lived in a
Christological key. God is present and active in the lives
of people. He is the God of the living. He is particularly
present as Holy Spirit and it is the reception of the Holy
Spirit which renews and gives life to a person. Indeed the
purpose of Christianity here, is to bring life, both a
future life in the new Zion but especially life here and
now (Pretorius 1987:38-41). This demands 'healing' as a
spiritual, physical, and psychological process; the kind of
healing which gives life as outlined above. It is a healing
which helps people to cope (Kiernan 1980:126). In the urban
situation, the African Independent Churches offer healing,
purification, strengthening to avoid danger, and the means
to deal with the difficulties of life in the new alien urban
environment. Healing is carried out through prayers calling
on the Spirit, through ritual and in particular through the
power of God working through the leader (Kiernan 1981:142).

Loewen points out that the African mindset will not
deny the efficacy of Western healing techniques and
medicine, but will maintain that they remain superficial as
they only deal with the physical and symptomatic (1976:411).
What is more important is the disturbance in the human
lattice or field of energy which is mankind as
relatedness-in-the-world (Cf. Setiloane 1975:31). Thus the
questions: who caused the disturbance? and why? are of
paramount importance. Western medicine never usually
considers this dimension and thus for the African is
unconcerned with the fundamental spiritual issue (Loewen
1976:411).

Daneel also emphasises that it is in responding to this
need that charismatic healing becomes the most attractive
feature of the African Independent Churches and the major

----

and could result in "isifo". "For a Zulu conceives good health not only
as consisting of a healthy body but as a healthy situation of everything
that concerns him. Good health means the harmonious and coordination of
his universe" (Ngubane 1977:27-28). The harmony is maintained by the
balance of the forces within the totality. These forces are present in
all being and have their source in God (Setiloane 1975:34).

factor in recruitment of new members. In a survey of several of these Churches, he determined that between 50-60% of all the members interviewed had joined because of experiencing healing (1983b:27).

Both Daneel and Kiernan point to the fact that part of the healing process comprises the necessary step of incorporating the person into a community, the Church, which provides for a sense of identity, belonging and security. In providing a conducive environment of interpersonal and social support the healing achieved is holistic and consequently, more effective (Daneel 1983t:29; Kiernan 1976:354). Kiernan illustrates how such a community also manifests itself liturgically in a kind of sacramental enactment of that which the Church is to be for the person, in the hostile environment of his daily life (1976:350-351 & 354).

Kiernan and Rounds study the phenomenon from a sociological and anthropological point of view and both come to the conclusion that people join these Churches and remain within them because they provide a means of helping the person to cope with the hostile environment in which they live (Kiernan 1981:142; Rounds 1982:83). On the personal level Rounds notes that at the time of their conversion 66% were in the midst of a crisis and the new religion provided a hope for the resolution of the crisis (1982:83). Ngubane has similarly pointed out that in his own experience, Catholics who become Zionists (the largest grouping of African Independent Churches) do so because they were sick and recovered after the Zionists prayed for them (Ngubane 1986:86).

Healing is also an experience of being harmoniously present in a community, and Kiernan suggests that the achievement of this aim, within the Zionist group, is the main task of its ritual (1976:354). In this way, a cohesive unity of society is created which can sustain the person by preparing him for the hostile world in which he finds himself as well as by purifying and healing him from the uncleanness and sickness it may infect him with during his working week (Kiernan 1976:342).

Both Rounds and Kiernan have studied the African Independent Churches as an urban phenomenon. Rounds notes that those joining the African Independent Churches are normally rural people recently arrived in the city, looking for a new way of coping with the pressures of life away from home and being integrated into the city with its foreign dimension of Western civilisation. In this way, they provide a bridge for the person to move from the rural to the urban reality (Rounds 1982:85). Kiernan also emphasises the urban nature of African Independent Churches:

The African Independent Church is being
increasingly viewed as a flourishing urban social
form wherein solutions are offered for specifically
urban problems.
...they cater for the needs of townspeople which
were formerly met by rural kin-groups and they
therefore provide a means of adapting to urban
life. [1981:142]

Daneel studies these Churches from a more theological
perspective and comes to the conclusion that "Much of what
we observe today in the Independent Churches concerns a
genuinely contextualised and originally African response to
the Gospel, irrespective of and unfettered by mission Church
influence" (1983a:58).

He suggests that they offer a holistic response to God
in faith which is most clearly manifest in long ritual
during which: "preaching, faith-healing, exorcism,
prophecies and pastoral care become interwoven activities in
an all inclusive event." Such an event is a celebration of
the effective presence of the "love and care of Christ alive
in their midst" (1983a:77).

Daneel agrees that for these Churches, salvation is
identified with healing understood as the restoration of
harmony and life, but he contends that the criticism that
they only understand salvation in terms of realised
eschatology, is misplaced since there also exists a clear
understanding of a future perspective to the eschaton
(1983b:40-41). Pretorius' research bears out a similar
conclusion (1987:38), whilst Mbiti has also pointed out that
the contribution of Christianity in Africa has been to
provide a future dimension to the African cultural
understanding of time (1971:60-61). It nevertheless remains
true that the concept of healing as realised eschatology:
receiving life, and thus salvation, now, is at the centre of
the African Independent Churches phenomenon. The insistence
of these Christians of living out the first part of the
Gospel is perhaps the most significant contribution they
offer to the universal Church[55].

----
55. By "first part of the Gospel", we refer to the ministry of Jesus
before the Transfiguration in which the emphasis is on preaching good
news and healing: Cf. Mk. 1,21-8,26; Mt. 4,23-16,12; Lk. 4,14-9,17.

3.1.3 Coping/Healing in the "White" Neo-Pentecostal Churches.

3.1.3.1 Appearance of the Phenomenon.

A Survey of the religious habits of whites in the Natal Province of South Africa conducted in 1983 has indicated that 8% of the population belong to the so called "Pentecostal" Churches and that a further 2% are currently exploring the possibility of moving from the more traditional Churches to these new Churches (Morran & Schlemmer 1984:222-229). The 1980 census of South Africa indicated that 8,5% of the white population were Catholics and that 13% belong to "Other Christian Churches" a term used by the censor to refer to the non denominational or non "mainline" Churches[56]. The same census revealed that 12% of the Asian population of the country are Christian and of this group some 37% belong to the "Other Christian Churches" group (Heyns 1986:779).

These figures give some indication of the numerical importance of the 'non-mainline' Churches in the country. There are many of these Churches in South Africa but almost all of them have their roots in the Pentecostal/Evangelical strain of Christianity. This strain of Christianity is extremely difficult to analyse because of the many groups and separate ecclesial communities which exist within it as well as the plethora of terms used to express self understanding and identity. "Apostolic", "Pentecostal", "Charismatic", "Born Again" and "Evangelical" are just some of the terms that these groups use to describe themselves. These terms are also used in different ways by the various groups who often ascribe different contents and meanings to them.

Several Churches in South Africa which have their roots in the turn of the century Pentecostal movement, have now become established denominations[57]. John Bond estimated that

---

56. The term "mainline" Church is currently used to refer to those historical denominations which represent the mainstream traditional expression of Christianity in South Africa such as the Roman Catholic, Anglican, Methodist and Presbyterian Churches (Cf. Morran & Schlemmer 1984:iv).

57. Anderson has pointed out that the Pentecostal Movement developed, out of an enthusiastic campaign of preaching and revival embarked upon in the United States during the latter part of the nineteenth century (1987:73). This campaign, often referred to as the Holiness Movement, laid great stress on the importance of divine healing as a central aspect of the Gospel. To this understanding, the Pentecostal Movement added the importance of receiving the gifts of the Holy Spirit, here and

in 1974 there were probably half a million Pentecostals in
South Africa most of whom belonged to one of four Churches:

-The Apostolic Faith Mission.
-The Full Gospel Church of God.
-The Pentecostal Protestant Church.
-The Assemblies of God.

Each of these four Churches is South African in origin
and was established after 1910 (1974:10-22).

During the 1960's and 1970's, the influence of the
Pentecostal Movement began to be felt in the established
mainline Churches when the so called "Charismatic Renewal"
developed within them. According to Lederle, this movement,
which was basically a "lay revivalist" movement, has spread
throughout the world and affected all Churches: Protestant
since 1958, Catholic since 1967 and Eastern Orthodox since
1971. The emphasis of this movement is also a felt
experience of the presence of God interpreted in terms of
"gifts of the Holy Spirit" (1986:61-62).

Both Anderson and Morran & Schlemmer have pointed out
that the Charismatic Renewal within the mainline Churches
has led to the "Pentecostal" experience being integrated
into the more affluent and established classes. Originally,
this was a phenomenon limited to the less affluent and the
emarginated sections of the population. In this way, the
phenomenon has become more respectable and is becoming, in a
certain way, culturally legitimate (Anderson 1987:73; Morran
& Schlemmer 1984:2).

During the 1970's and the 1980's, a further dimension
has been added to this movement with the emergence of the
"New" or Neo-Pentecostal Churches. These Churches retain the
basic tenets of the Pentecostal and Charismatic movements
but they have added a new dimension to their message: the so
called "Prosperity Gospel".

The first of these Churches appeared in 1979 when a
former Catholic, Ray McCauley, returned from the "Rhema
Bible Training Centre" of Kenneth Hagin in the United
States. By 1985, McCauley's Johannesburg Church had over ten
thousand members and had spawned a whole series of "Rhema"
Churches throughout the country. In that year, the Rhema
Churches formed an association of New Charismatic Churches
together with the "Goeie Hoop Bedieninge" of Nickie van der
Westhuizen and the Hatfield Christian Church of Edmund
Roebert. This association, "The International Fellowship of

----

now manifest in felt experience, and especially through the gift of
"Tongues", glossolalia. For this movement, the experience of being "born
again" in the Spirit was a necessary sign of being a Christian.

Christian Churches" (IFCC), represented 216 Churches and 110 000 adherents in 1986 (Anderson 1987:74). Whilst this association is the largest, it is by no means the only grouping of what we shall term the "New Churches" (Cf. Morran & Schlemmer 1984:iii). Another organisation, Christian Fellowship International also represents a significant grouping of these Christians (Anderson 1987:74).

The members of these Churches are predominantly white. In the Durban area it has been estimated that the racial breakdown of membership is of the order of 80% white, 20% asian, 8% "coloured" and 2% black (Morran & Schlemmer 1984:56). These figures probably reflect the national situation although the high concentration of Asians in the Durban area would tend to skew this figure upwards.

Clearly a growth to over 100 000 members between the years 1979 and 1986 in the predominantly urbanised and mainly white group indicates the emergence of an important religious phenomenon in our time.

3.1.3.2 Doctrine.

3.1.3.2.1 The Doctrine of Classical Pentecostalism.

John Bond, who is a minister in the Assemblies of God Church, indicates that most traditional Pentecostals believe in a two stage spiritual experience (1974:15):

> 1. Salvation by faith alone in the redemptive work of Jesus.
> 2. A second experience of the Baptism of the Holy Spirit.

Neither of these stages is elitist and both are open to all Christians. The main indication of the second stage is the experience of glossolalia. Pentecostals also distinguish themselves by emphasising enthusiasm in worship, preaching which deals with the problems of personal life and a felt experience of the Spirit. "Pentecostalism supplies an immanence of the supernatural which takes the individual out of the closed system and opens heaven to his experience" (1974:17-19).

3.1.3.2.2 Doctrine in The Charismatic Renewal.

The Charismatic Renewal movement referred to earlier has introduced these tenets of Pentecostalism into the mainline Churches. Their doctrinal position is more complex as there is an attempt at synthesis between the Charismatic experience and the existing tradition. Lederle suggests that the denominational Charismatics, which is by far the biggest grouping, recognise the charismatic movement to be essentially compatible with their tradition but enriching it[58].

3.1.3.2.3 The "New" Independent Churches.

The New Churches referred to earlier remain in the Pentecostal tradition but have added a further dimension: the so called "Prosperity Gospel". The idea that God bestows prosperity on his followers was already preached in the revival movements even as early as 1930 (Morran & Schlemmer 1984:5). It has been popularised since then through evangelists such as Oral Roberts, Kenneth Copeland and Kenneth Hagin. Hagin is the founder of the Rhema Church in the USA and many leaders of the New Churches in South Africa have ties with his organisation, "Kenneth Hagin Ministries". Hagin has produced books and pamphlets with titles such as "Godliness is Profitable" and "You can have what you say" (Verryn n.d.:25-28).

These Churches are fundamentalist in their interpretation of Scripture and in the affirmation of its authority. The Prosperity Message proclaims that it is God's will for people to prosper. God promised Abraham many blessings including material prosperity and every "born again" Christian is heir to this covenant and has the right to expect God to fulfill his side of the covenant as long as two basic requirements are made (Morran & Schlemmer 1984:6):

1. That Jesus is accepted as Saviour and Lord.

---

58. Lederle (1986:65) says that the charismatics within the mainline Churches can be divided into three groups:
    a) Neo-Pentecostal Group.
    They retain a two stage pentecostal spiritual experience and consider glossolalia as a necessary sign of the baptism of the Holy Spirit.
    b) Sacramental Group.
    The Baptism of the Holy Spirit is interpreted as the release of the Spirit already received in the sacraments of Baptism and Confirmation.
    c) Integration Group.
    The Charismatic experience is integrated into the daily Christian life. This group recognises that the experiential is part of the Christian faith and would naturally expect the Charismatic experience to be available to anyone professing the Christian faith.
Clearly these categories overlap one another and are suggested by Lederle only to facilitate understanding of the phenomenon.

2. That the person lives according to God's laws as
outlined in the Bible and not according to the natural
laws of this world which are infected by the power of
Satan.

Prosperity is understood in the full sense of material,
spiritual, physical and mental prosperity. Kenneth Hagin
outlines four steps to get what the Bible promises (Morran &
Schlemmer 1984:9-11):

1. Say it. (Put what you want into words or "put words
to your faith").

2. Do it. (Put action with your faith).

3. Receive it. (Act as though it is already yours).

4. Tell it. (Tell others so that they may believe).

According to this teaching, poverty, illness and death
are the curse of the law from which believers are freed.
Poor and sick people are poor and sick because they have not
fulfilled the spiritual requirements and are thus under the
power of Satan. All suffering is caused by Satan and can be
removed through faith and healing.

3.1.3.3   The Coping/Healing Ministry in Pentecostalism and its Manifestation in the New Churches.

It is our contention that the Pentecostal and
Charismatic Churches are responding to the need, which
people have, to experience the power of God in their lives.
In particular, they are helping people to find a means of
coping with their existential situation. In analysing and
reflecting on this phenomenon we wish to limit ourselves to
the New Churches. By this we mean those which have appeared
during the 1980's. In doing this we recognise that they
represent only one segment of Pentecostalism and of the
Charismatic Churches and share only some teaching and
practices in common as we have already outlined. In limiting
ourself to this group we also acknowledge that they
represent a more radical strand within Pentecostalism.
Nevertheless we choose them because it is precisely this
group of Churches which is having the most phenomenal growth
at this time and thus clearly responding most effectively to
the perceived need of its constituency.

Anderson adopts a very sympathetic position with regard
to these Churches. He says that they allow people to
experience the "already" of salvation:

But is not the good news the fact that Christ has *potentially* won the victory for us over sin and all forms of human misery; and that he desires us to enjoy the fruits of that victory here and now - including forgiveness of sin, peace with God and man, and his material provision? [1987:80-81]

He considers that the New Churches have a more holistic view of salvation as opposed to the dualistic view often ascribed to the more traditional Churches. The phenomenon is thus analogous to that of the African Independent Churches with which he explicitly links it (1987:81-82).

Other authors however are much more critical. Takatso Mofokeng, replying to the article of Anderson suggests that the appearance of an "American Dream" style Prosperity Message in post 1976 South Africa places the Prosperity Message at the opposite wing to the message of Black Theology and contradictory to it. The issue here is that of the arrogation of wealth and political power by whites in South Africa (Mofokeng 1987:84-86). Since the Soweto riots and killings of 1976, blacks in South Africa are questioning the right of white people to the exclusive possession of wealth and power. Black Theology is at the forefront of theologically legitimizing this process. On the other hand, the Prosperity Message is providing a theological legitimisation for the prevailing status quo and the further acquisition of wealth and power by whites.

Several other authors concur that these Churches are helping the privileged to discover a theological legitimacy for their lifestyle[59]. Morran & Schlemmer conclude that these Churches are in fact helping to resolve the fears and anxieties of white people in South Africa regarding the future of the country[60]   When the stress is placed on

----

59. Cf. Verryn 1983. See also the bibliography of this work together with that of Morran & Schlemmer 1984 for other books dealing with this theme, especially in the international arena.

60. There is a fundamental insecurity manifesting itself amongst white people today based on the implicit knowledge that sooner or later major changes will have to occur in the society. The main perception is that these changes will be to their disadvantage and so should be staved off for as long as possible. It would also seem to be true that most whites are of the opinion that the present system is the best possible in South Africa. Nevertheless this same system is under a major ideological, theological and political attack at the present time. This attack is referred to by the South African Government as a "Total Onslaught" on South Africa. The search is therefore underway for an effective ideological and theological justification for the present situation in order to reinforce the will of the threatened community. The theological issue is important in South Africa because religion continues to hold a prominent position for the majority of the population, both black and white.

wealth as a sign of God's blessing and poverty as a sign of the presence of Satan, it is clear that the position of the white group is given a certain theological support. Such a theological vision also helps remove any sense of guilt which white people may feel for the current crisis situation (1984:183).

What is also interesting is the fact, already noted, that these kinds of Churches normally appeal either to the poor or emarginated. In their current enthusiasm to join these Churches, we believe that this group of people, ostensibly rich and powerful, is in fact acknowledging a new status in South Africa: that of becoming increasingly emarginated. It is an emargination within the country, from the population as a whole, as well as an emargination from the human community at large, within the international arena.

Through the use of community forms of worship and an emphasis placed on strong interpersonal and group relatedness within the Church community, the New Churches provide a safe, warm healing experience of community within which people can become whole and thus face the evil of the world (Morran & Schlemmer 1984:181). In this way, people are being made to feel "happier, healthier, wealthier, more positive and more powerful as a result of joining the new churches." (Morran & Sclemmer 1984:174). They help resolve the fears and insecurity of the white group which considers itself highly threatened.

However the same authors point out that the cost and consequence of belonging to such groups is, in the end, a loss of the fullness of humanity. They point out that the New Churches particular *modi operandi* do not finally help people to deal with life in a fully human way. They are Authoritarian and Anti-Intellectual, discouraging rational and critical thinking by providing a simplistic vision of reality where problems are translated to the supernatural. Such an approach, they indicate, can have severe negative psychological consequences (1984:175-176). They also tend to provide short-cut, consumer oriented approaches to religion with the accent on instant gratification, which refuses to take account of the deeper problems of human life, especially regarding social issues and the structural causes of the human condition (1984:177-178). In this way the phenomenal increase in influence over the white population which these Churches are experiencing can have consequences which mitigate against the full development of the human person on the level of psychological maturity and social responsibility. Consequently, the salvation that the New Churches offer and the morality that they propose seems to be defective in terms of the Gospel and the Christian faith as a whole (Verryn 1983:28).

69

We conclude that these Churches are offering dimensions of salvation as realised eschatology which are not found in the traditional Churches. This is their popularity and it is on this level that they provide a challenge for the traditional Churches. At the same time, there are profound distortions of the Christian message in the salvation they offer, which is often only a palliative curing only the symptoms of the disease. Now the symptoms are important as indicators of the sickness. If the sickness is not cured and the symptoms are annulled, the consequences could be tragic. The New Churches may be serving to augment this danger.

3.2. THE PASTORAL PLAN
OF THE CATHOLIC CHURCH IN SOUTHERN AFRICA.

3.2.1 Introduction: The Emergence of the Pastoral Plan.

The 1974 Synod of Bishops on the theme of Evangelisation had important consequences for the African Church. During the Synod, the 39 Bishops from Africa and Madagascar met together every week. At the end of the Synod, they issued an important declaration on "Coresponsible Evangelisation" in which they indicated the importance of the African Church becoming more fully responsible for its own destiny and less dependent on the European Churches which had originally founded the African Missions. This declaration also introduced the key themes of "Communion" and "Coresponsibility" as the mode within which the African Churches were to fulfil their mission today. The stress in this document was on the fact that the time has now arrived when the "young Churches of Africa and Madagascar must take over more and more responsibility for their own evangelisation and total development[61]. The thrust of the document was a recognition of the fact that the African Churches were no longer in the phase of being the "Mission territories"of the European "Elder" Churches but that they had now become local Churches in their own right and had to take full responsibility "to set the priorities of pastoral planning and activity, to take the initiative called for by the mission of the Church (Fitzgerald & Hurley n.d.:51).

The response to this declaration by the Sacred Congregation for the Doctrine of the Faith was extremely positive[62]. Particular encouragement was given to the development of theological research conducted by African Theologians opening the way for a theological pluralism "in the unity of the faith and in fidelity to the authentic tradition of the Church" (Fitzgerald & Hurley n.d.:54).

In South Africa the spirit of these initiatives had already been operative earlier in 1974 when at the July plenary session of the SACBC, the bishops commissioned a

----

61. The quotes come from "Coresponsible Evangelisation. Declaration of the Bishops of Africa and Madagascar present at the 4th Synod of Bishops." Rome October 20 1974 being Chapter 10 of Fitzgerald, J.P. (Archbishop) and Hurley, D. (Archbishop) *World Bishops Meet: Report on the Rome Synod.* Pretoria: SACBC, n.d.

62. Archbishops Fitzgerald and Hurley refer to it as a "historic document opening the way to a new era in growing together for the Church in Africa" (n.d.:54).

study on the local needs of the Church in South Africa under the theme "Evangelisation today in South Africa" (ETSA). A widespread consultation of the Church was undertaken by Fr. C. Hulsen S.M.A. and by December 1976 a "tentative final report" was drawn up (SACBC 1984:1).

The major thrust of Fr. Hulsen's work was to emphasise the present reality of the Church in South Africa as an overwhelmingly black Church. Following from this, he concluded that "the Church's general policy, her pastoral planning, her new structures, her prayerful study and attention should be clearly determined by the needs and spiritual and social demands of her black majority" (Hulsen 1976:180). In this regard, he suggested that the principal problem that the Catholic Church faces is that it is "Structured along lines that are foreign and white in a country which is overwhelmingly black" (Hulsen 1976:113)[63].

The ETSA report was, however, superseded by two developments which occurred during 1976. The first was the incident in Soweto in June of that year when student protests led to the killing of hundreds of young people by the South African Police. The preoccupation of the Conference moved to this matter and a "Statement on the Current Situation" was issued in February 1977 affirming "that in this matter we are on the side of the oppressed" and committing the Church to work for peace through justice (SACBC n.d.3:1). The second development was a "Declaration of Commitment on Social Justice and Race Relations within the Church" made at the plenary session. In this declaration the Bishops committed themselves to a Pastoral Consultation to bring together Catholics from all over the country in order to determine, together with the Bishops, "a policy on Church life and Apostolate but not on doctrinal or canonical matters" (SACBC n.d.3:2-6).

This Pastoral Consultation was carried out in two stages. During 1979, a consultation was made amongst the various groups and organisations within the dioceses regarding their own needs and priorities. These findings were then summarised in a base document used at the Interdiocesan Pastoral Consultation, which brought together 178 delegates representing Catholics of South Africa, Namibia, Swaziland and Botswana. The consultation made over one hundred recommendations in six basic areas of

---

63. Here Fr. Hulsen quotes the document "Oblate Orientations" produced by the Provincials of the Southern African Region of the Oblates of Mary Immaculate. The document was drawn up to indicate priorities for Oblate mission and to attempt to formulate common orientations for the six O.M.I. provinces within the region.

Cathechetics, Liturgy and Sacraments, Lay Responsibility and Formation, Justice, Family Life and Youth (SACBC 1980:48-53).

The magnitude of the task indicated by this consultation emphasised the necessity of developing a consultative ongoing process of Pastoral planning. So from 1983 onwards, preparations were made to develop an effective Pastoral Plan which would respond to the complex needs of the South African context. In order to help the Church reflect on this issue, a "Pastoral Working Paper" was drawn up and submitted to parishes, movements, religious communities, and individuals for their reflection. This process continued during 1984 and 1985 and from the comments and responses received, the following major points emerged (SACBC 1987:4):

a) There is a need for a Pastoral Plan in the Church in Southern Africa inspired by the understanding of the Church which emerged in Vatican II.

b) This understanding of the Church must be related to the realities of life in Southern Africa.

c) There should be a key theme for the Pastoral Plan and this can be formulated as "Community Serving Humanity"

d) that the basic element in the plan must be FORMATION i.e. the evangelization of all people in the Church : bishops, priests, Religious, laity, adults, youth and children in terms of the vision expressed by the theme.

The Pastoral Plan was formally introduced to the Church in 1987 by means of a Pastoral Plan Kit which was sent to all dioceses and through them to all parishes in the country. Each parish was guided through a series of reflections on the theme and asked to adopt or reject the plan, giving reasons. The matter was then discussed at diocesan synods held towards the end of 1987. As a result of these deliberations, the Bishops Conference formally decided to commit the Churches of Southern Africa to following the Pastoral Plan from Pentecost 1989 onwards.

3.2.2 The Pastoral Plan and its Theme.

Pastoral planning is the means that the Church uses in order to develop methods and means of realising its mission in South Africa (SACBC 1987:2). However, it wishes to be something deeper than a mere list of techniques and methods. Its basic purpose is to attempt to "improve the quality of

Christianity in the Church" (SACBC 1987:4). It does this in two basic ways. The first is to provide a vision of the kind of Church we wish to be. This vision is summed up in the theme "Community Serving Humanity". The second is by means of a process of Evangelisation and Renewal which will enable the Church to live this vision.

The theme chosen for the Pastoral Plan: "Community Serving Humanity" expresses the goal towards which the Church wishes to move during the coming years. It is based on a synthesis of two factors:

1) The Views expressed by the various groups, parishes, and individuals making up the local Church during the Pastoral consultation.

2) The Vision of the Church which has become universal since Vatican II.

It is thus a synthesis of the local and Universal dimensions of the Church: an attempt at Inculturation.

3.2.2.1 Community.

The South African Church wishes to become a community both as a response to the division of Apartheid and as a rejection of the image of the Church as a "Mass of Individual Consumers". But it also wishes to become the image and manifestation of true community which finds its source in the love which is the Spirit binding Jesus to the Father (SACBC 1987:15-16). South African society is built upon the division and difference between groups of people. Consequently, one of the principal thrusts of the Pastoral Plan is to overcome these divisions and to look for ways in which community can be built. At the same time, the Plan wishes to take into account the diversity between the various groups and cultures in the country, attempting to build a unity built upon "diversity in a community bound together by love" taking into account the "need to give much fuller reign to local customs in the Church" (1987:10).

3.2.2.2 Serving Humanity.

The South African Church also wishes to become a "Serving Community" (SACBC 1987:16), carrying on the mission of Jesus who came not to be served but to serve (Mt. 20,28). Serving humanity implies a special commitment to those in desperate need: "whose humanity is degraded or denied in some way or other" (SACBC 1987:17). It is a commitment to building a better world. In the South African context the restoration of human dignity takes on a particularly important role in the ministry of service. The mission of service is not so much one of doing things for people rather than striving to create a society in which the fullness of human dignity is respected. The Church must "preach and practice and fight for the dignity of all people. It must oppose all systems and laws that enforce ...injustices" (SACBC 1987:10).

3.2.3 The Pastoral Plan and its Method.

If the aim of the Pastoral Plan is clear: that the Church should become a "Community Serving Humanity", the question remains: how do we move from our present situation to that of being in the process of becoming a community serving humanity? "How can our aspirations become a reality" (SACBC 1987:19)?

This question was placed before the whole Church of South Africa through the parish structures by means of a "Pastoral Plan Kit" which was sent through the dioceses to all the parishes during 1987. The kit comprised a Workbook and posters providing a method of enquiring into the basic question. Eight themes were presented for discussion. One concerned the key theme of "Community Serving Humanity" and the others considered ways of developing a sense of the Church as Community as well as the issues of human dignity and service.

These meetings were animated by teams of leaders who had been trained on the diocesan level in the process of animation of others through participation. The training was experiential in nature, involving going through the process themselves and then reflecting on this experience in order to see how to lead others through a similar process. The method of the meetings encouraged discussion and participation by all present. This concept of formation by participation, rather than learning by being told, was central to the process. These teams were then sent throughout the diocese to lead parish representatives through the same process thus helping them to learn the same animation process by experiencing it themselves. These representatives then went back to their own parishes to animate the same process with their own co-parishioners.

In this way, the central team gave birth to new teams trained in the same method. These latter were then sent to the parishes where they presented the same discovery process to the parishioners. More teams were consequently trained within each parish. A major feature of the process was the fact that each meeting was always animated by a team working together and never by one individual.

The process outlined above is clearly a formation process: it is formation by participation and formation within groups. This process of formation by community, in community and to community is essential to the method of the Pastoral Plan.

3.2.4 Building Community: Three Methods Commended by the Pastoral Plan.

The Pastoral Plan carries with it a requirement for re-evangelisation and a deepening of faith within the Church. This is the meaning of the phrase "to improve the quality of Christianity in the Church" (SACBC 1987:4). The process of formation required to do this must occur within the liturgy, through cathechesis and through Gospel sharing groups (SACBC 1989:20-22). However, three particular methods are highlighted as means of increasing the sense of community and of the serving Church. These are: the creation of Small Christian Communities; the "Renew" process (infra 3.2.4.2) and Multiple Task Groups (infra 3.2.4.3).

3.2.4.1. Small Christian Communities.

In South Africa as elsewhere in Africa, the Catholic Church has opted for Small Christian Communities as the means living faith. They are seen as a privileged way of living the aim of the Church as a Community serving Humanity. They are a means of "initiation into a spiritually richer and more vigorous Christian Life in which the laity assumes its full and rightful role in many aspects of the Church's mission" (SACBC 1987:20).

Small Christian Communities are not new to the South African Church. In 1978, the SACBC decided in its plenary session to promote them and about one sixth of the parishes in the country have established them, with varying degrees of success, whilst others are in the process of taking steps to have some kind of structure similar to them.

The Pastoral Plan considers Small Christian Communities to be: "The most intensive form of community building in the parish ... but this is also a demanding form" (SACBC 1989:37). They are described as follows:

> They are neighbourhood communities; they are intended to be permanent; they meet weekly in members' homes by rotation; they are based on Gospel sharing and on communal action; they form a network coordinated through the Parish Pastoral Council. All Catholics, including members of associations and movements, are invited to

participate. There is no blueprint or universal form for such communities. Experience has shown that they flourish equally well in urban and rural areas. [SACBC 1989:37]

Small Christian Communities operate in many different ways using different methods and with different programmes and procedures. As a community open in faith to the promptings of the Spirit, it is very important that this should be so. This openness to a diversity of styles programmes and functions is particularly important in the South African situation where the cultural context from one area to another is so great. The different groups often have differing priorities, experiences, languages, attitudes, styles and needs. At present, residential Apartheid means that most parishes are either exclusively White or exclusively Indian or exclusively Black township dwellers etc. It is only in the rural areas where there is a little overlap between the groups but even this is usually minimal.

3.2.4.2. The "Renew" Method.

For people who have yet to discover the value of community, it is suggested that pre-formation is given to help people to discover one another and the value of sharing and working together. The "Renew" program developed in the United States as a programme for parish renewal in evangelisation and community development, is one means of doing this[64]. The "Renew" program is described as a:

> spiritual renewal process to help parishioners develop a closer relationship with Christ, to make an adult commitment to Jesus as central in their lives and to open them to the power of the Holy Spirit so that they become more authentic witnesses. [SACBC 1989:38]

----

64. The Renew process needs to be promoted on a diocesan basis with as many parishes as possible participating. First a diocesan Team of leaders is trained and this team is responsible for training parish teams who are then responsible to share the renew process with as many people as possible. The process happens over a period of two and a half years and is based around a series of five intensive six week periods called 'seasons'. Each season has a theme as follows:

Season 1 (Sept-Oct: Year 1)	The Lord's Call.
Season 2 (Lent: Year 2)	Our Response to the Lord's Call.
Season 3 (Sept-Oct: Year 2)	Empowerment by the Holy Spirit.
	(with a large emphasis on Social Justice)
Season 4 (Lent: Year 3)	Discipleship.
Season 5 (Sept-Oct: Year 3)	Evangelisation.

The entire "Renew" experience is a conversion process and parishioners are invited to join in in four ways:

-In the Sunday Liturgy.
-In the family by means of take home materials.
-Through large group activities.
-through Small Sharing Groups.

The final way is intended to be the deepest form of participation and in this way, it is hoped that a familiarity with sharing and interacting on this level will form the bridge to a later introduction of Small Christian Communities (SACBC 1989:39). The "Renew" program is considered to be most helpful for the more urbanised and Westernised communities although the Archdiocese of Durban, for example, has adopted the program as the means of fulfilling the Pastoral Plan in all of its parishes (Archdiocesan Bulletin June 1988:39).

3.2.4.3 Community Building Through Multiple Task Groups.

This method of community building is also intended to help parishes where the value of community relationships is not well developed in the culture. It is based on bringing people together in small groups in order to perform certain tasks. The great advantage of the method is that people easily see the need for the group because there is a concrete task to be performed. Its dangers are twofold. First, that it does not involve all the people of the parish in some form of group but only those who are keen to be involved in tasks. And secondly that the focus of the group must eventually change from a task mentality to a relationship mentality if the groups are to become community building. For this step to occur, relationship training is needed in the task groups almost from the beginning. The South African Bishops Conference has prepared training and programmes for groups who want to follow this method (SACBC 1989:39).

3.2.5 Ongoing Training Methods.

Once the various parish communities have been established, it is important to look at the different types of method which are available to help them continue. Many groups begin with the initial enthusiasm of launching but then do not continue. A lack of formation and of programming is usually the problem. With this in mind a series of eleven methods has been collected by the Lumko Missiological Institute in South Africa. Most of these are based on the famous *See Judge Act* method of Cardinal Cardijn. They do provide means which the communities can use should they so wish and which animators and trainers can have available to help groups struggling in this area[65].

Whilst methods can prove useful it is also important that each group develop its own style of being a Small Christian Community. This will depend on the people, the community, the needs of the area, and especially on the inspiration the group receives in faith-response to God's call. For this reason methods can never be imposed, but only suggested.

3.2.6 Conclusion.

The Catholic Church in South Africa finds itself on a threshold of a new phase of its existence as it attempts to follow God's call discerned in a process of reflection, prayer and discussion over the last ten years. Clearly, the launch of a new initiative of this nature, on a National level, is a major undertaking. The project is only in its early phases and so it is not yet clear what the impact of this Pastoral Plan will be either in the Church in Southern Africa or on the society. Nevertheless, the initial response of people seems to be very enthusiastic with, for example, several thousand people attending the launching ceremony in the Archdiocese of Durban where many groups seem to have already been formed (Archdiocesan Bulletin November 1989:103-105). This enthusiasm is reflected also in the approach of the hierarchy. The Pastoral letter of the

----
65. Some methods are more difficult than others. They are listed below in sequence from the simpler to the more complex:

1. The Neighbourhood Gospel Group (NGG).
2. Look-Listen-Love.
3. Group Response.
4. Parish Search.
5. Our Journey Together (RCIA based).
6. Amos Programme.
7. See-Judge-Act.
8. Theo's (or animators) method.
9. Social Analysis.
10. The Psycho-social Method (PSM).
11. Vamos Caminando.

Cf. Nolan, A. & Broderick, R. 1987:89.

Archbishop and his auxiliary read at the launching,
indicated the hope which the plan has engendered in the
local Church.

> We look forward to parishes being intensely
> involved in the building up of their small
> communities with much prayer and commitment: loving
> one another, encouraging one another, meeting one
> another across the old unhappy unchristian
> barriers which separate peoples in South Africa;
> finding in   one another true expressions of the
> presence of Jesus working in us for the salvation
> of the whole world.

> That is our dream.   That is our hope. That is the
> reason for the excitement of an Archbishop and a
> Bishop both now old in years, but renewing their
> youth as the Archdiocese renews itself in prayer
> and worship; in faith hope and love; in community
> spirit and Christian Service[66].

---

66. Hurley, D. & Khumalo, D., "A Pastoral Letter from the Archbishop
and Bishop Dominic Khumalo for Pentecost Sunday 14 May 1989" in *News
Bulletin, Catholic Archdiocese of Durban May 1989 pp. 40-41.*

CHAPTER FOUR

INTERPRETATION OF THE PHENOMENA:
THE SEARCH FOR A HERMENEUTIC KEY

4.1 Introduction.

In the previous two chapters, we attempted to describe
the five phenomena emerging within the Community of Faith in
South Africa. In this chapter, we wish to enter more deeply
into the analysis of these phenomena in order to try to
understand something of their internal structure and their
relationship one to the other. We are now more concerned
with understanding and interpreting the phenomena we have
described and so our efforts will be directed towards the
search for a hermeneutic key. This will help draw out the
meaning of the phenomena within the particular context of
their manifestation. An analysis of the meaning of these
phenomena will provide us with valuable indications
concerning priorities for action and in the final part of
the work we hope to indicate some priorities for mission
and, in particular, evangelisation, which result from our
interpretation.

There are obviously many interpretive keys which could
be used to relate, understand and interpret these
phenomena[67]. We do not pretend that the options we make are

----

67. Clearly our phenomena can be interpreted in terms of various models
or keys, each of which would help illuminate a particular dimension of
the overall problematic. An economic key would indicate the way in which
these phenomena might be interpreted in terms of the economic relations
and transformations occurring in the country. An anthropological key
would attempt to explain how these phenomena are linked with the
development of cultural identity and social transformation occurring in
the country today. Models reflecting the various ideological positions
within the country could also be developed to explain the data. Leatt,
Kneifel and Nurnberger have tried to analyse some of the various ways of
understanding and interpreting the social reality in the country in
their book *Contending Ideologies in South Africa*. Cape Town: David
Philip, 1986. Our work concerns the religious phenomena as such and for
this reason we have opted for a theological key. Nevertheless, two other
interpretative keys did suggest themselves to us before we made our
decision. A Scriptural key would attempt to relate what is happening
today more directly to the Scriptures in an attempt to identify more
clearly, how the Scriptures speak to us today. Itumeleng Mosala has
attempted to do this for Black Theology in his book *Biblical
Hermeneutics and Black Theology in South Africa today*. Grand Rapids:
Eerdmans, 1989. A more exotic Psycho-Spiritual key was inspired by John
Welch's Jungian interpretation of St. Teresa's "Interior Castle" in his
book *Spiritual Pilgrims*. N.Y.: Paulist, 1982. in which the phenomena
could be interpreted in terms of the Spiritual Journey the People of God

exhaustive or exclusive. Nevertheless we do believe that they will provide us with important theological insights which could affect future pastoral planning especially with regard to strategies for evangelisation.

Our reflection will begin with an initial attempt to order and to relate the phenomena in terms of the predictions and interpretations of some South African authors. From there we will pose three initial presuppositions for our own interpretation. These relate to the affirmation of the role of the Holy Spirit, the primacy of the Kingdom of God both as 'telos' and as a present reality and, thirdly, to the affirmation of the validity of the experience of the Christian Community as the subject of the unfolding experience of truth which the phenomena articulate.

We will attempt to construct our hermeneutic key on the basis of these presuppositions. It is thus a theological key in the sense of "Fides Quaerens Intellectum". We will then investigate the two main prevailing theological models found in the literature: the model of "Contextualisation" and that of "Inculturation". From this we hope to indicate why we see both these models as being important in giving a fuller understanding of the phenomena we have studied.

Finally, by means of conclusion, we hope to draw some indications regarding the priorities for evangelisation in the South African context so that the signs we have discussed may be seen and followed.

4.2 Reflection on the Data.

We have already noted that the five phenomena are related amongst themselves (supra 1.4; 2.1.1.2; 2.2.4.4.3; 3.1.1). There is an historical priority in the three theologies in that we have noted that both Prophetic Theology and African Theology are partially dependent on Black Theology in the South African context, even though both have roots which predate the emergence of both Black Consciousness and Black Theology (supra 1.4; 2.1.1.1). We have also noted the importance of Black Consciousness as a turning point in the understanding of the journey to liberation in South Africa (supra 2.2.3.1). In this regard, the six theses of Manas Buthelezi, presented at the Congress on Mission and Evangelism in Durban during March 1973, are significant. In this statement, Buthelezi pointed out the dependence of the future of the Christian faith in South

----

is called to make in order to reach the Kingdom of the Father.

Africa on "How the Gospel proves itself relevant to the existential problems of the black man" (1973a:55) and that the future of evangelism in South Africa was "tied to the quest for a theology which grows out of the black man's experience" (1973a:56). We contend that the way in which the phenomena we have treated have manifested themselves and are related amongst themselves demonstrates the veracity of Buthelezi's prophetic words.

In treating each of the five phenomena we have tried to describe something of the internal structure of each one, indicating some of the important themes that each is attempting to cope with. In this section we will be more concerned with indicating the principle essences of each phenomenon and the relationship between these. It is for this reason that we will attempt to use models in order to understand something of the totality. From this we hope to show that the phenomena, properly understood, indicate some important priorities for the evangelisation process in the current situation.

In the first place we consider the three theologies we have described. We have already noted that these deal with issues such as the identity of the ecclesial community, its experience of faith in the situation it finds itself, its self understanding and the content of its evangelisation (supra 1.4). These theologies are a reflection that the ecclesial community makes on its experience in the South African context.

Our analysis began with Prophetic Theology because we believe that it provides us with a thread of historical continuity, situating the events of the past twenty years with that which went before. We have tried to show with Corijn that a diachronic process of mutation and growth has been going on within the Church since its arrival in the country (supra 1.3; Cf. also SACBC 1984:18-33). For our purposes we highlighted the importance of the post war period during which the South African Church has emerged more clearly with a South African identity and agenda. In the section on Prophetic Theology we tried to indicate in what way Prophetic Theology stands in the tradition of the more liberal ideological framework of the 1950's and 1960's even though it also stands in radical discontinuity to it. The contribution of Prophetic Theology is that it indicates the essential nature of the Church in its relationship with political power and authority. Prophetic Theology is demonstrating the need for a healthy tension between the Ecclesial Community and the State, in which the Church recognises its responsibility to read the signs of the times and exercise a critical role within society, thus opening the society in hope towards a better future.

If Prophetic Theology provides the framework of continuity with the past, and helps to situate the present phenomena within a historical process, then it is Black Theology which provides the moment of discontinuity which allows the process to move onto a different level of understanding. It is for this reason that we have treated Black Theology as the second phenomenon.

Black Theology carries with it three moments which are also the major essences of its identity. The first of these is a "Consciousness Moment" in which people discover their humanity and move from being non-persons (non-whites) to persons: subjects of their own history. The second is a "Liberation Moment" which is a conscious commitment to participate in the transformation of the world, seen as non-world inhabited by non-persons, into a human world inhabited by human persons. The third is a "Dialogue Moment" in which communication on a person to person (or community to community) basis is established in place of the previous relationship of master to servant (powerful to powerless). Whilst there is clearly a certain sequencing of these processes in the order we have indicated, these moments are also ongoing and concurrent within the total phenomenon.

In the South African situation, the phenomenon of African Theology is a manifestation of the call of the future possibilities for the South African Ecclesial Community rather than a return to past traditions. More than the other two phenomena, African Theology is helping to establish the framework and groundwork of the future identity of the Ecclesial Community in South Africa. This may seem to be a paradox since African Theology has often been accused of lacking an eschatology and of being too tied to the past[68]. However, the South African authors are insisting on a new understanding of African culture reflecting African patterns of understanding in todays world (supra 2.3.2 & note 31). It is in describing some of the parameters of such an updated and evangelically transformed African culture that African Theology in South Africa is indicating a vision towards which the Community of Faith is called to move[69].

----

68. This fact has been born out in research into African Independent Churches which are the most prevalent locus of a lived African experience of faith at the present moment. M.L. Daneel, who has studied these Churches in some depth suggests that the criticism that these Churches only understand salvation in terms of realised eschatology, is misplaced and that there also exists a clear understanding of a future perspective to the eschaton(1983b:40-41). Pretorius' research bears out a similar conclusion (1987:38). Mbiti has also pointed out that the contribution of Christianity in Africa has been to provide a future dimension to the African cultural understanding of time (1971:60-61).

With regard to the pastoral phenomena discussed, it would seem that three powerful symbols of pastoral involvement or ministry are emerging. They provide an indication of the kind of means required to participate, create and manifest the Kingdom of God within South Africa. These are the symbols of healing, community and service (supra 3.1.1; 3.2.2). Indeed these fundamental biblical and theological categories have emerged now precisely because of the needs within this particular context. If an individual, a community or a nation is sick then healing is necessary and whenever Jesus came upon such situations he responded. The large numbers of people who are seeking religious forms of healing clearly demonstrates the sickness of the society. Their needs are easily exploitable and this is the danger within the healing ministry. However it is just as dangerous (perhaps even more so) to deny the existence of the disease when its symptoms abound or to deny the validity of this ministry when Jesus himself spent the first part of his own ministry involved in it (Cf. Mk. 1,21-8,27 & Mt. 4,17-16,12). It is our contention that the ministry of healing should be a central mode of the Church's activity at this time.

The emphasis on separation and division within our country has been responded to by an emphasis within the Church on the development of serving communities of faith: communities formed with the aim of serving the humanity of South Africa. This is the meaning of the Pastoral Plan of the Catholic Church. The emphasis on building communities of faith is a clear sign for us at this time. This is particularly true within the Catholic Church where the shortage of clergy and different structural emphases has led to the emergence of large and usually impersonal parish structures especially in the urban areas. Clearly, the implementation of the plan will demand the growth of lay participation and leadership within the Church and help the move away from a basically clerical model of power and authority (supra 3.2.2). Setiloane's concept of "relatedness" (supra 2.3.4.2) can provide a powerful category of understanding for the development of such communities. That the communities are serving communities determines the fundamental direction of the Church's priority at this time. We are moving away from a period of internal reflection, in which valid categories of identity as 'Church in a modern world' were the priority, towards a more involved phase of concern for the transformation of the

---

69. Here I use African in the sense which Mogoba stresses. He takes it to mean all those who are born in Africa and committed to it whatever their ethnic, historical and cultural roots may be (1985:16).

society and culture within which we live. The fundamental relationship that the Community of Faith wishes to cultivate with the society it finds itself part of is one of service: ready to respond to the needs of the people in the prevailing context of crisis.

The themes we have described above form the framework within which the South African local Church is called to live, function and grow at this time. They are themes which have emerged from our phenomenological analysis and thus are part of a lived reality in South Africa now. In order to have a more comprehensive understanding of their meaning, we now wish to enquire into the way they fit together as part of a totality or as part of one ongoing process. This is the search for a hermeneutic key. Before this however we wish to indicate some theological presuppositions which will form the background of our search.

4.3 Theological Presuppositions.

We restrict the search for a hermeneutic key to the theological field since we wish to understand the meaning of the phenomena within the horizon of the faith experience of the Ecclesial Community. We accept that the theological interpretation is only one of several which could have been used[70]. The theological key also provides us with a basis for drawing valid conclusions regarding the continuing movement of the Ecclesial Community on its journey to the Kingdom of God: a journey which is primarily one of faith and grace and not readily intelligible outside this horizon (Cf. 1Cor.1,17-25).

Before entering into our search for a hermeneutic key it seems appropriate to begin by explicitating three presuppositions which form the framework of our discussion and whose validity is not discussed here. The first of these is an affirmation of the presence of the Holy Spirit as an

----

70. We have already noted the various possibilities of hermeneutic key (note 68). Here we wish to indicate the variety of approaches which have been taken by South African authors. Villa-Vicencio refers to his analysis as "a sociological and theological reflection on the social function of religion" (1988:6). Motlhabi refers to his book as a Social Ethical analysis of black resistance to Apartheid (1988:vii). Leatt, Kneifel and Nurnberger speak of a "soft phenomenological" description of ideologies in South Africa together with a "theological critique of the ideology as concept" (1986:ix). Mosala attempts to develop a specific Biblical Hermeneutics upon which a true Black Theology can be based (1989:3). Finally Bührman tries to link Jungian psychological categories to the experience of healing in traditional African Religion in an attempt to understand them (1986:16).

active presence animating and motivating the Christian community. This is a presence which can be discerned and which consists in calling the Community of Faith to obedience to the Father's will and supplying it with the power (grace) to fulfill that will (GS 11;LG 48; Comblin 1979:42-48;105-107; Lopez-Gay 1988:68). This same Spirit forms the basis of the dynamic which conducts the Church along its journey towards the Kingdom of the Father (Dom. Viv. 26).

The second presupposition concerns the primacy of the Kingdom of God as the fundamental goal towards which the Holy Spirit moves us. Participation in the process of realising or actualising the Kingdom of God in the world forms the fundamental mission of the Church to the world (LG 5; GS 45; Fullenbach 1987:1-6).

Our third presupposition affirms the validity of the experience of the Christian community: the Church understood as: "the community of faith and hope: one, holy, catholic and apostolic" (LG 8). By this we mean that it is the Christian community which is the subject of the experience of faith and which exists in a constant relationship with God who cares for her, constantly speaks to her and nourishes her[71]. The Christian community, the Church, is the destination to which the signs are directed and thus this community is most able to interpret them in terms of the covenant relationship which exists in Christ. This presupposition wishes to affirm that the Church is in a particular relationship with God which is the ground of the "experience of faith" as well as the condition of the possibility for discernment of the meaning of the experience.

These three presuppositions indicate the parameters which determine the horizon and structure of our reflection and the boundaries within which our hermeneutic key is required to operate. In this way, we hope to interpret the process which lies behind the phenomena which are manifesting themselves and which have formed the subject of the first part of our analysis. This process can be described in terms of its basis or "ground", its aim or finality (telos) and its subject. The presuppositions we have made relate to these three parameters. Thus the

---

71. We have already indicated that in the South Africa context it is impossible to limit the discussion to the Catholic Church (supra 1.2.2). Our presupposition regarding the Church or Ecclesial Community is in terms of the fuller interpretation given to LG 8 without any denominational specification being made. This is not to deny that denominationalism within the Ecclesial Community in South Africa does not play a role. But such a role would be the subject of another enquiry and is not considered here.

"ground" within which the key functions is the enduring
presence of the Holy Spirit guaranteed by Christ during this
time of the Church (Jn. 14,16-17): the subject of our first
presupposition. The aim, or goal to which the process is
directed is the Kingdom of God, the concern of our second
presupposition. Finally, the subject of the process is the
Community of Faith: the Church, which is the object of our
third presupposition.

4.4 The Search for a Hermeneutic Key.

A general survey of the literature indicates two major
keys which are used in order to understand phenomena such as
those we have indicated. In the english speaking and mainly
protestant ethos the favoured term seems to be that of
Contextualisation. Here the stress is on the "word"
understood as a "text" which speaks within a "context" which
may have historical, cultural socio-economic and political
dimensions. The term more favoured within the Catholic
Church is Inculturation and this term has been widely used
in Papal addresses and more formal magisterial statements
(Cf. George 1987). The emphasis in the Inculturation model
is on the Community of Faith: the local Church and the
process it undergoes as it roots itself into a particular
culture. The difference in emphasis leads to a difference in
approach and we shall eventually argue that the two
approaches are complementary offering a synchronic and
diachronic explanation of the situation.

4.4.1 Contextualisation as Interpretive Key.

4.4.1.1 Contextualisation amongst South African Authors.

A survey of the South African literature reveals that
this term and its derivatives such as Contextual Theology,
context, Contextualisation of the Gospel and so on, is used
almost exclusively to describe the process of relating the
Gospel or the Christian faith to the South African
situation. Boesak prefers to call Black Theology a
Contextual Theology as this is a more embracing term than
indigenous Theology or cultural Theology. Contextual
Theology means a response to the Gospel within the
particular context of the world which includes the cultural
dimension as a part (1977:14).
de Gruchy also feels that the word Contextual is more
appropriate since it "conveys most adequately what it
signifies" (1986:13). The context is more than a cultural

one in South Africa since the country finds itself in a particular historical situation of crisis with demands being made especially on the level of social justice and transformation (1986:14).

Bosch defines Contextualisation as "relating the Gospel message to the entire existential context of a group, in which the cultural element may be playing a very significant role" (1976:83). For this reason, the term Contextualisation is wider and allows the Gospel to speak in a more holistic way to all the life issues within a particular society. In a later article, Bosch indicates the necessity for the Gospel, as text, to engage in "creative and dynamic dialogue" with the context. Such a process which occurs within a hermeneutic circle is one which gives the Gospel life and meaning and without which the text remains abstract (1983:493).

The image for Contextualisation is "word". It is word as text which is always found within a particular context. Villa-Vicencio suggests that the text is "shaped" by the context and in this way given form, and presumably, meaning (1987:9).

Nolan tries to get to the meaning of Contextualisation by means of another approach. For him the priority is the notion of "Gospel". By definition, this is always Good News and so the Gospel today in South Africa must be just that: something new which is told to people to bring them joy. Nolan suggests that the words in the Bible are not the formal content of the Good News today but rather indicative of the "shape" which such Good News should take. Thus the kind of things which Jesus said, which were good news to the people of his time, indicate the kind of things that his apostles need to be preaching to the people of this time (1988:8; 25-28). The continuity of the Gospel is not found in the letter (content) of the Scriptures but in the spirit (shape) of them. The "shape" remains the same since the Scriptures are fixed in a canon but the content will always vary so that the Spirit may inspire the apostles to preach good news today. Nolan maintains that the Gospel has always been contextual and has no fixed verbal content. "The Gospel is shaped by what the Bible says about God but its content is the latest news regarding the events of God in South Africa today" (1988:16).

In order to determine the Good News today, Nolan says we must read the "Signs of the Times" through the human events we can see (1988:19). Thus Contextualisation is "the process of discovering what the Spirit is saying to the Churches in our context today" (1988:27).

4.4.1.2 Contextualisation in the International Arena.

Contextualisation is one of the burning issues today in theology and there are a variety of meanings and understandings put on the term as the previous section has indicated in the limited field of South Africa. It is clearly impossible to enter fully into this problematic here and we wish only to provide some indications as to the directions the studies are taking.

Lutzbetak (1981) and Haleblian (1983) who follows much of his analysis with some significant differences, have attempted to put order in the confused field of Contextualisation by analysing the various models available. Lutzbetak identifies three models of the method of Contextualisation which operate today: the Translational Model based on Bible translation theory and developed by Charles Kraft; the Dialectical Model of Robert Schreiter and the method of Liberation Theology (1981:39). Haleblian rejects the latter as a model since he considers it to be a Contextual Theology itself rather than the model of a method of Contextualisation. Haleblian is more concerned with the process of how the Scriptures legitimately enter into a context (1983:95). He sees the essential issues as: "how to deal with syncretism, the limits of Contextualisation, the core of the Gospel and hermeneutics" (1983:103). Any methodology of Contextualisation must deal with these issues. Lutzbetak also relates Contextualisation to the Gospel but speaks of a blending of understandings within the Church of both the Gospel and the world (1981:39). This difference in vision would also seem to explain their disagreement regarding Liberation Theology. We agree with both authors, and with Schreiter himself, that whilst the model of Kraft is useful on the level of linguistic accommodation and conceptual translation it is weak in finding a place for all the richness of culture (Lutzbetak 1981:44-47; Haleblian 1983:105; Schreiter 1985:8). It would be difficult to see how Kraft's model could explain Contextualisation in terms of either Bosch's definition or Nolan's understanding as indicated above. We will thus consider the model of Robert Schreiter to see to what extent it can be used as a hermeneutic key in the South African situation.

4.4.1.3 Schreiter's Model of Contextualisation.

Schreiter's model is referred to as a Dialectical Model by Lutzbetak (1981:48) and as a Semiotic Model by Haleblian (1983:106). Schreiter maintains that all theology is contextual (1980:267) and that its purpose is to help clarify the self-understanding of an already evangelised community (1980:269). The theology that such a community constructs is a "Local Theology" and he adopts this term as his basic concept (1985:6). He sees the major task of theology as helping to establish the "identity of the Christian community" as well as helping to "clarify the values, establish the beliefs, locate the ills and chart the trajectories of a community" (1980:272). The construction of a Local Theology is "the dynamic interaction among the Gospel, Church and Culture" (1985:22).

Central to Schreiter's model for the construction of Local Theology is his concept of culture. He adopts a very wide definition of this term considering it to be "the concrete context" in which the process of the emergence of a Local Theology occurs (1985:21). He understands culture in terms of two main factors: cultural identity and social change (1985:22). By considering also the latter, he is able to include the socio-economic and political factors which would not fall within the scope of the meaning of culture for the South African authors.

When Local Theology is dealing with the area of cultural identity then two major issues are investigated. The first concerns the determination of the boundaries which mark off or distinguish a particular social group from those around it. The second deals with the development of a cohesive world-view within which the group can understand itself (1985:44).

When issues of social change are being considered, the theological problematic revolves around the new set of circumstances which have occurred and which need to be incorporated, transformed or rejected by the community (1985:44).

Schreiter also emphasises the necessity of a holistic approach in the understanding of culture which is brought to theology. If this is not done there is the danger that a reductionist theology will emerge which interprets faith in terms of one or two central factors but which neglects other important areas. As an example of this he cites the initial failure of Liberation Theology in Latin America to understand the role which popular piety had in helping people to cope with oppression (1985:43).

Schreiter's model of culture is semiotic and extremely complex. The culture is analysed in terms of the structures of meaning within it. These structures are made up of a network of sign systems which relate to one another through a complex semantic system. Cultural analysis is the attempt to determine the laws governing this system. The basic unit in the analysis of culture in the semiotic system is the "culture text" which is a combination of signs which carry cultural meaning. The texts can be as simple as a single sign, verbal or non verbal, carrying a particular meaning such as a gesture or an object like a wedding ring. It can also be extremely complex and itself be made up of many smaller culture texts such as a liturgy or ritual. Semiotic analysis seeks to analyses these culture texts in terms of the signs which make them up as well as to study how they interact in order to create and determine new meaning regarding identity and change within the culture.

4.4.1.4 Schreiter's Model and the South Africa Phenomena: An Encounter.

We have seen that Schreiter's model has three components: Gospel, Church and Context (which he calls culture). We now need to see if this model can be used to adequately describe and interpret the five phenomena we have considered.

The first priority would seem to be the ability to adequately describe what we mean by the term "context". We have already indicated that there is a wide understanding of this term amongst the South African authors. However it does seem possible to indicate some parameters. South Africa is clearly undergoing rapid social change. It is a society in which people experience oppression and control in a variety of ways based on skin colour and socio-economic status. It is a society where the division between the poor and the rich is very marked where there is much economic hardship and suffering counterposed to great wealth in a totality perceived as relatively wealthy (at least by African standards). It is a very violent society both on the physical and the psychological level. It is a dangerous place to live. It is also a society in which cultural identity, practices and mechanisms are going through a process of rapid change and where the traditional modes of coping with life are no longer effective. It is a society where there is much anxiety concerning the future and future identity. It is a society in crisis: a crisis which has built up as a result of a conflict of understandings, wills and power regarding a future vision of the society and the process of arriving there.

The question of cultural identity and its analysis in terms of identity formation boundaries and world view seem particularly useful in the interpretation of the consciousness moment in Black Theology and the search for a new cultural identity being made by the African Theologians. The critical stance of Prophetic Theology towards those in authority is also often made in terms of a shared world view, in this case Christian morality.

On the other hand, the call for involvement in a process of liberation being made by both Black Theology and Prophetic Theology can be interpreted in terms of the categories of social transformation as outlined by Schreiter's model. On a different level the Coping/Healing ministries are also clearly responding to this same category and can be interpreted within it as we have already indicated (supra 3.1.2.2 & 3.1.3.3). The same can be said for the Pastoral Plan.

The context is thus very complex and whilst much of the foregoing can be placed into Schreiter's categories of cultural identity and Social Change we would suggest adding a further category of 'crisis factors' to indicate the particularity of the present moment. By a category of 'crisis factors' we refer to a situation where the tensions in society are so great as to produce a limit situation. When the normal social and cultural mechanisms which help people to deal with the tensions in their lives are no longer able to cope with the pressures, a limit situation is introduced. The category of Kairos as understood by the Kairos Theologians and by Nolan would only fit in such a special category (supra 2.1.3). These authors lay great stress on the importance of discerning the presence of the Holy Spirit through the signs of the times and it would seem that the category of 'crisis factors' is best interpreted in this mode of discernment of spirits. Consequently we would add a further parameter to our model of Contextual Theology : that of the Holy Spirit. Thus our model has four parameters:

1. The Gospel: in its various understandings as outlined above.
2. The Holy Spirit as guide, especially in a prophetic sense, during the crisis situation where socio-cultural limits are strained and a Kairos is precipitated.
3. The context: following the broad definition of Bosch and specifying this in terms of the following categories:
    -cultural identity
    -social change
    -crisis factors.
4. The local Community of Faith: subject of the Local Theology and responsible for it.

We believe that such a model which is basically that of Schreiter with some nuancing can interpret the five phenomena we have described.

4.4.1.5 Application of the Model to the Phenomenological Analysis.

4.4.1.5.1 The Gospel in South Africa.

One is inclined to agree with Nolan that the Gospel to be preached in South Africa today has to be good news and that evangelisation cannot consist in a mere restatement of the words of Scripture (1988:25). However, we believe that it is precisely the process of Contextualisation of the Gospel which seeks to do that. Contextualisation of the Gospel is that part of the process of evangelisation concerned precisely with letting the Scriptures become good news within a particular context as well as word of life for the Christians within that context. Nolan and the other South African authors are in fact attempting to indicate how the words of Scripture are to be used and understood within the total process of evangelisation in South Africa today. The phenomena we have discussed indicate the major dimensions and factors which comprise the Good News in South Africa today. We indicate below the specific contribution of each phenomenon.

> From Prophetic Theology: the discernment, identification and naming of sin especially in its social mode as it deforms the day to day existence of people within the society. The proclamation of a special time of the Holy Spirit as a Kairos which calls for a qualitative leap forward in faith towards the vision of a future proclaimed in hope. The importance of challenging those in authority and with power to measure up to the demands of God's word.
>
> From Black Theology: the affirmation of the value and dignity of all people especially the poor and most abandoned and in particular those who are specifically dehumanised by the prevailing socio-political norms and laws: black people. The affirmation that salvation is concerned with human liberation in this world and that the mission of Christians is to be involved in this process.
>
> From African Theology: the affirmation that all people in a community or culture are basically related in an integral whole and that the future calls us to a cultural unity which will respect differences and not absolutise the particularities of this or that group.

From the Coping/Healing Ministry: that our particular context calls for a special emphasis on this ministry of healing and on the joy and good news of the first part of the Gospel (Cf Mk. 1,21-8,26).

From the Pastoral Plan of the Catholic Church: that the Gospel Values of building community and being of service to the society as a whole have assumed particular importance in the present context and indicate priorities for the Church's mission.

These are not the only factors that could be drawn from our phenomenological analysis but we believe that they do indicate the major priorities regarding how the Gospel is contextualising itself in the South African situation.

4.4.1.5.2 The Holy Spirit in South Africa.

Clearly the preceding category of "Gospel" is linked to this one since it is the Holy Spirit who renders the Gospel intelligible (Cf. Jn. 15,26; 14,26; 16,8.). Nevertheless we include the Holy Spirit as a parameter of Contextual Theology because we think that He provides the key to a clearer understanding of the crisis moment: the Kairos. We agree with Nolan and the Kairos theologians that there is a particular prophetic presence of the Spirit during crisis moments which calls the Community of Faith to new responses and new experiences. The Holy Spirit is found within the "Signs of the Times" and his presence is discerned through faith. In the Kairos he calls for a quantitative leap forward in faith which may demand a radical break with past understandings and practices since the ordinary responses may no longer be adequate. This is the reason for the Kairos (supra 2.1.3). We maintain that it is difficult to understand the emergence of the five categories without taking into account this special category.

4.4.1.5.3 The Context.

We accept Bosch's definition of context as "the entire existential context of a group" (1976:83) because it is wide enough to include all the dimensions of the phenomena we have investigated. It obviously needs to be elaborated and specified in terms of more workable categories. Amongst these we have identified a socio-economic and political context within which both Black Theology and Prophetic Theology are working. We have also shown that the

Coping/Healing Ministry also operates as a response to this category as both Rounds and Kiernan as well as Morran & Schlemmer demonstrate (supra 3.1.2.2; 3.1.3.3).

Together with Lutzbetak and Schreiter we also identify a cultural context and in particular the search for cultural identity with which African Theology is concerned as we have indicated. However we find it difficult to accept Schreiter's understanding of culture which also includes social change and which for him seems to be synonymous for context. There are two reasons for our difficulty. The first relates to the normal understanding of the word within the South African situation where it has been the victim of Apartheid ideology and has acquired a negative connotation not found elsewhere. The word is almost exclusively understood in an ethnographic category. Consequently, the category of social change would be obscured within the South Africa debate on culture. The second objection however concerns the transcultural nature of many of the parameters of social change. One only has to think of economics which has a scientific as well as a cultural dimension. Some of the laws of economics are as verifiable as any of those of physics and chemistry although clearly others depend more on values and so are more closely linked with culture. Consequently it would seem confusing to put the transcultural empirical dimensions together and call them culture when they are really not that group dependent. The vaguer concept of context seems more able to support an interdisciplinary approach which Contextual Theology should always attempt to be.

Finally there is the dimension of "Crisis" as the context which deals with limit conditions. Here we are concerned with a context where the evils of oppression, unnecessary suffering, injustice, fear, anxiety and violence build up so much that a limit condition is reached and a tension is set up within the context which becomes too great for the existing social, cultural, political economic and religious mechanisms to deal with. Consequently a new paradigm is required and much of the energy of the community is required to be expended in order to discover this.

4.4.1.5.4 The Local Church.

The subject of this whole process and indeed of the phenomena we have described is the Community of Faith : the Ecclesial Community : the local Church understood in the sense we have outlined (supra 1.2.2). The phenomena emerge as they do precisely because there are people of faith united by earthly bonds of community as well as transcendental bonds of communion. This community searches to understand its faith, manifest as its lived experience in the world. In coming to understand its faith, the community determines its identity as well as its program for action. It is only the Community of Faith which can render the experience of the Spirit and the Gospel intelligible. Thus the local Church is the locus of Contextual Theology and the guarantee of its authenticity.

4.4.1.6 Strengths and Weaknesses of the Contextualisation Model.

We stated at the beginning of this work that it would be an exercise in Contextual Theology. We consider this hermeneutic key to be the best way of interpreting the phenomena we have considered. It's greatest strength is that it has the possibility of focus. Thus one is able to both narrow and broaden the context in order to consider the Gospel and indeed the local community in terms of particular contexts: cultural, socio-economic etc. In this way it is possible to develop particular theologies somewhat in the way we have tried to do with our own divisions of Prophetic Theology, Black Theology and African Theology. This division is not our own but was suggested by the division made by the editors of the book *Hammering Swords into Ploughshares,* (Mosala, I. & Tlhagale, B. 1986:xii-xiii).

The major limitation of the Contextualisation model is that it tends to be static in its understanding. It is a synchronic approach indicating themes trends, priorities and preoccupations at a particular time. This limit is obviously imposed by the meaning of the concept "text" and "context" which tend to be static rather than dynamic in character. Clearly Schreiter would not agree with this judgement since his model allows for a diachronic dimension in terms of his category of social change. Social transformation occurs through a process of dialectical change as new meanings are either incorporated or transformed. However we have already noted the complex nature of Schreiter's model and he gives little indication as to how this process occurs (Cf. 1985:72-73).

To indicate the importance of the diachronic dimension we wish to explore the Inculturation model especially as it has been outlined by Arij Roest Crollius. We have already indicated that Inculturation is the current preferred term in Roman Catholic literature and an investigation of the application of this interpretative model to our data would seem valuable.

4.4.2 The Inculturation Model.

Schreiter indicates that there is a lack of consistent terminology in the theology which is attempting to relate the Gospel, the faith and the Church to the local context (1985:4-6). He registers his preference for the term "Local Theology" as a general term covering the various models but eventually opts for the contextual model as the "most important and enduring in the long run" (1985:16).

Roest Crollius had already referred to this confusion some time earlier, restricting himself to the relationship between the Community of Faith and the culture it encounters (1978:722-724). Roest Crollius adopts the term Inculturation to describe the process of this relationship through time and compares it to the process of "Enculturation" which he understands as the "learning experience by which an individual is initiated and grows into his own culture" (1978:725).

The subject of the Inculturation process is the local Church and Roest Crollius indicates three moments in the Inculturation process: Translation, Assimilation and Transformation. "Translation" is a process of acculturation: a cultural encounter in which the local Church is first evangelised by missionaries coming from a different cultural background in which there is an attempt to translate the missionaries' faith experience, understood in terms of their own cultural categories, into the cultural categories of the local people. "Assimilation" refers to the process of reflection which the local evangelised Community of Faith attempts to make as the faith takes root within the new culture. "Transformation" refers to the moment in which the local Church, securely rooted within its cultural context, now attempts to transform that culture, attempting to bring it closer to the vision of the Kingdom of God, affirming and developing what is of value whilst continuing the struggle against evil. The transformation moment is thus a moment of renewal for the culture which seeks to find the presence of the Holy Spirit within the particular cultural expression of the faith (Roest Crollius 1978:733).

The value of Roest Crollius' model is that it is diachronic. It analyzes in more depth the historical process which goes on within the life of a local Church and which provides it with a local Christian tradition as well as a vision of the future to which it is called to be oriented.

Some of the dimensions of the phenomena we have studied are interpreted more clearly in the diachronic model. In particular we wish to consider the contribution of those Black Theologians who are beginning to speak in terms of the development of a new culture within South Africa and are beginning to look to African Theology in order to find indications for the direction which this process should take. We have already pointed out that the concept of culture is being considered in terms of a unifying horizon towards which society could ideally move (supra 2.3.4.1). The hope of Tlhagale and others for the emergence of a new, fully African culture corresponds to the beginning of Roest Crollius' transformation moment in the Inculturation process. At this time it remains an eschatological value: a "not-yet" calling for actualisation. It is a goal understood in the sense of the vision of the Kingdom of God expressed in local contextual categories. The society is being called to move towards this goal.

Tlhagale maintains that a rational critical approach is essential to the development of culture in the South African situation for only here is the tendency to absolutise cultural myths and ethnic values countered. This, he contends, is absolutely necessary in order to create an open, culturally plural society (1985:35). Without the dethronement of these myths and absolutisations, true communication and hence true liberation is rendered impossible (Tlhagale 1983:121).

> Culture becomes a stumbling block to intergroup
> communication when the functional aspect of one
> particular culture is overemphasised or raised to
> the level of an absolute. [1983:113]

Within the parameters of Roest Crollius' Inculturation model, the five phenomena are mainly manifestations of the assimilation phase. We have already indicated that since the second world war, the Church has been attempting to root itself more deeply into the South African soil and much of what we presented in our first part indicates the way in which the Church is attempting to become South African and to assimilate the culture. However the call of the African Theologians represents something new. The African Theologians may prefer to refer to themselves as Black Theologians but they represent a new dimension of Black Theology which is taking African Theology more seriously and the call for a genuine "African Theology" is significant here. This represents a shift towards the transformatory phase.

It might be argued that the premises of, for example, Prophetic Theology or even, for that matter, of Black Theology, are also calls for the transformation of the society in terms of the Gospel and therefore form part of the transformation phase. There is obviously some truth in such an assertion but the major issues with which these theologies concern themselves, relate to the sinfulness of society in terms of both its history and the present context. In this way, they are calls to redeem society from its sin rather than for the transformation of cultural values and identity. It is only to the extent that these theologies present a vision of society in terms of the Kingdom of God: a future horizon towards which the community is called to move, that they become transformatory. The same thing can be said with regard to the Pastoral Plan of the Catholic Church. It too presents a vision of society and even of a culture, which is not yet actualised (SACBC 1984:6-16). However it does this in a very general way with little link to the South African problematic. In the final document, however, the vision is more clearly explicitated:

> Our plan is to be a Church which is a true community where all feel they are brothers and sisters. Our plan is to be a Church which serves all people helping them to a life which is truly human, truly formed in the image of God. [SACBC 1989:5]

These two aims are then elaborated within the document. Clearly the crisis situation is such in South Africa that the process of being freed from the social structures of sin and evil is still the priority. Nevertheless the beginnings of the emergence of the kind of society we wish to be as well as the beginnings of outlining the cultural parameters necessary for such a society is an important step forward and one where much work will have to be concentrated in the near future. The Inculturation model of Roest Crollius is important here because it helps to indicate this particular priority in a way which the Contextualisation model does not. For this reason the two models are complementary helping us to render the phenomena we have considered more intelligible within a more holistic framework.

CHAPTER FIVE

CONCLUSION

EVANGELISATION IN THE SOUTH AFRICAN CONTEXT

The Inculturation model we have discussed, as well as the comments of the African Theologians regarding the necessity of moving towards a new cultural matrix in South Africa, lead naturally to the question of evangelisation. In the transformation moment, the local Church begins to actualise more clearly its responsibility to challenge the culture and the society to become more Christian. Whilst the assimilation moment is more interiorised and the evangelisation that goes with it also more inward (Cf. EN 15), the transformation moment is more extroverted. An interiorly purified and evangelised Church confidently confronts the society and its culture with the values of the Gospel and the living presence of the Holy Spirit which it has already experienced in its own molding process (EN 18).

The five phenomena we have considered help to specify the particular content of the evangelisation process which is called for in our particular context. Prophetic Theology indicates that the Gospel we should be preaching is one of hope based on a radical commitment to the presence of the Holy Spirit in the Kairos. This presence is demanding that those in positions of power and authority within the country be challenged regarding their own culpability for the crisis situation which has developed and their current obligation in truth and justice within it. It is also calling for the adoption of a prophetic stance for justice and truth against the disvalues of fear and force currently operative.

Black Theology is saying that the Gospel is a message of consciousness, liberation and communication. Consciousness implies the preaching of the worth and dignity of every human person. Evangelisation for liberation implies the witnessing to a society freed from the structures of sin and evil which were set up to maintain white privilege, which have led to the oppression of black people and which have resulted in the dehumanisation of all people. Evangelisation for communication implies the building up of a society which is a true community where there can be true communication between brothers and sisters equal before God and one another. It is also saying that the key to this process is the particular initiative which God is wanting to take with the black man in South Africa who, at this juncture, has become the major catalyst of the process.

African Theology is indicating the importance of preaching a vision of the Kingdom of God which is called to take root and become immanent in the South African context. It is a vision which takes into account the particularities and the richness of a society which God wishes to redeem and allow us to live in. It is a culture in which many of the values we already hold (but which we guard from one another in fear) are called to become the common patrimony of all as they are impenetrated by the vision of the Gospel and the power of the Holy Spirit. It is a call to move towards a commonality of culture which will respect the plurality of expressions without absolutising any particular one: a truly catholic culture.

The growth in the Coping/Healing Ministry is reminding us that Jesus' preaching of the Gospel was accompanied by many signs, the most common of which was healing those who were sick and possessed. When the society is sick then the people need a doctor and Jesus healed all those who asked him. In this time a crisis, the ministry of healing will form an essential dimension of the evangelisation process as it did in the crisis time of Jesus himself.

Finally, the Pastoral Plan of the Catholic Church has indicated two key Gospel values which assume particular importance at this time. The building of community and the mission of service within the greater society indicate the way in which the local Community of Faith will be able to authentically fulfill its role as an evangelising community seeking to transform the society and the cultures which comprise it. "Community serving humanity" provides a model within which the Gospel may be effectively preached today as well as an important content of such preaching. Through its emphasis both on preaching the Word and suggesting a program for effectively building up the Kingdom of God in South Africa, the Plan is evangelisation in the full sense of the Church's understanding (EN 24).

In summary, then, Evangelisation today in South Africa means a particular priority being given to the following:

Proclaiming and actualising the dignity and value of each person and culture within the society.
Healing the victims of the crisis we find ourselves involved in by calling upon the power of the Spirit to be realised.
Actively working to build community amongst all Christians and within the society.
Naming and confronting the evil existing within the structures of society and indicating the presence of structures of sin which trace their roots to

the actions of men, especially those responsible for the exercising of all forms of power and authority.

Proclaiming and actualising a Salvation understood in terms of a liberation from the structures already specified by means of the commitment and involvement of the Community of Faith within the society.

Adopting a modality of service towards the society in which we live.

Moving towards a new Culture in South Africa transformed by the Gospel in which all people and groups are respected and none absolutised. A society in which neither people, ideas, systems or possessions are allowed to appropriate the role or position of God.

Living in an attitude of hope that the Lord is determined to create this future and build his kingdom amongst us.

The challenge confronting the Church in South Africa today is clearly immense. But the resources she has to draw on are greater. Since the victory over evil is already won in Christ we know that God's kingdom will eventually prevail. The challenge before the Community of Faith in South Africa, is to play its part in actualising the vision. It is a challenge that the Lord has made to all men since he first called Abraham and like Abraham it will depend on our faith in his power.

BIBLIOGRAPHY

AA.VV.
1983   *Inculturazione: Concetti, Problemi, Orientamenti*   Roma:
           Centrum Ignatianum Spiritualis.

AA.VV.
1985   "South Africa Today: The Kairos Debate." various articles
           Journal of Religion in Southern Africa 55:42-57.

Anderson, A.
1987   "The Prosperity Message in the Eschatology of Some New
           Charismatic Churches." *Missionalia* 15:72-83.

Anderson, G.
1974   "A Moratorium on Missionaries." in Anderson, G. & Stransky,
           T.,eds., *Mission Trends No. 1,* pp. 133-142. N.Y.: Paulist.

Barrett, D.
1979a   "African Christianity (Contemporary)." in *Encyclopedic
           Dictionary of Religion,* pp. 62-64. Washington: Corpus.

Barrett, D.
1979b   "African Independent Church Movement." in *Encyclopedic
           Dictionary of Religion,* pp. 64-66. Washington: Corpus.

Barrett, D.
1988   "Status of Global Mission, 1988, in Context of 20th
           Century." *International Bulletin of Missionary Research*
           12:7.

Bevans, S.
1985   "Models of Contextual Theology." *Missiology* 13:185-202.

Biko, B.S., ed.
1972   *Black Viewpoint.* Durban: Sprocas.

Biko, S.
1978   *I Write What I Like.* San Francisco: Harper & Row.

Blenkinsopp, J.
1969   *The Men Who Spoke Out: The Prophets.* London: Darton Longman
           & Todd.

Boesak, A.
1977   *Farewell to Innocence: A Socio-Ethical Study on Black
           Theology and Power.* N.Y.: Orbis.

Boesak, A.
1984   *Black and Reformed.* N.Y.: Orbis.

Boff, L. & Boff, C.
1984   *Salvation and Liberation: In Search of a balance between
           Faith and Politics.* N.Y.: Orbis.

Bond, J.
1974   "Pentecostalism in the Pentecostal Churches." *Journal of
           Religion in Southern Africa* 7:10-22.

Bosch, D.
1976   "Crosscurrents in Modern Mission." *Missionalia* 4:54-84.

Bosch, D.
1977   "The Church and the Liberation of Peoples." *Missionalia* 5:27-34.

Bosch, D.
1983   "An Emerging Paradigm for Mission." *Missiology* 11:485-510.

Bosch, D.
1984a   "Mission and Evangelism: Clarifying the Concepts."
            Zeitschrift für Missionswissenschaft und Religionswissenschaft 68:161-191.

Bosch, D.
1984b   "The Scope of Mission." *International Review of Mission* 73:17-32.

Bosch, D.
1986   "Process of Reconciliation and demands of Obedience - Twelve Theses." in Tlhagale, B. & Mosala, I.J., eds., *Hammering Swords into Ploughshares,* pp. 159-172. Basingstoke: Marshall Pickering.

Brueggemann, W.
1983   "Trajectories in Old Testament Literature and the Sociology of Ancient Israel." in Gottwald, N., ed., *The Bible and Liberation,* pp.306-321. N.Y.: Orbis.

Brown, W.
1960   *The Catholic Church in South Africa.* London: Burns and Oates.

Bryant, R.
1975   "Toward a Contextualist Theology in Southern Africa." *Journal of Theology for Southern Africa* 11: 11-19.

Bucher, G.R.
1976   "Toward a Liberation Theology for the 'Oppressor'." *Journal of the American Academy of Religion* 44:517-534.

Bühlmann, W.
1977   *The Coming of the Third Church.* N.Y.: Orbis.

Bührmann, M.V.
1986   *Living in Two Worlds.* Willmette, Illinois: Chiron.

Buthelezi, M.
1973a   "Six Theses: Theological Problems of Evangelism in the South African Context." *Journal of Theology for Southern Africa* 3:55-56.

Buthelezi, M.
1973b   "African Theology and Black Theology: A Search for Theological Method." in Becken, H-J., ed., *Relevant Theology for Africa,* pp. 18-24. Durban: Lutheran Publishing House.

Buthelezi, M.
1973c   "The Theological Meaning of True Humanity." in Moore, B.,
             ed., *Black Theology: The South African Voice,* pp.93-103.
             London: Hurst.

Buthelezi, M.
1976a   "The Christian Presence in Today's South Africa." *Journal of
             Theology for Southern Africa* 16:5-8.

Buthelezi, M.
1976b   "Daring to Live for Christ" in Anderson, G. and Stransky,
             T., eds., *Mission Trends No 3,* pp. 176-180. N.Y.: Paulist.

Chikane, F.
1985   "The Incarnation in the Life of the People of South Africa."
             Journal of Religion in Southern Africa 51:37-50.

Coe, S.
1976   "Contextualizing Theology" in Anderson, G. and Stransky, T.,
             eds., *Mission Trends No 3,* pp. 19-25. N.Y.: Paulist.

Comblin, J.
1979   *The Meaning of Mission.* N.Y.: Orbis.

Cone, J.
1969   *Black Theology and Black Power.* N.Y.: Seabury.

Cone, J.
1970   *A Black Theology of Liberation.* Philadelphia: Lippincott Co.

Connor, B.
1988   *Where are we Going as Church.* Hilton, South Africa:
             Cornerstone.

Corijn, D.
1987   "The Catholic Church and Apartheid." in *OMI Documentation.*
             153/87. Rome: Oblate Information Service.

Daneel, M.L.
1983a   "Communication and Liberation in African Independent
             Churches." *Missionalia* 11:57-93.

Daneel, M.L.
1983b   "Charismatic Healing in African Independent Churches."
             Theologia Evangelica 16:27-44.

Daneel, M.L.
1984   "Towards a Theologia Africana? The Contribution of
             Independent Churches to African Theology." in *Missionalia*
             12:64-89.

de Gruchy, J.W.
1979   *The Church Struggle in South Africa.* Grand Rapids:
             Eerdmans.

de Gruchy, J.W.
1986   *Theology and Ministry in Context and Crisis.* London:
             Collins.

de Gruchy, J.W. & Villa-Vicencio, C., eds.,
1979   *Resistance and Hope.* Grand Rapids: Eerdmans.

de Gruchy, J.W. & Villa-Vicencio, C., eds.,
1983   *Apartheid is a Heresy.* Cape Town: David Philip.

de Haas, M.
1986   "Is Millenarianism Alive and Well in White South Africa?"
            Religion in Southern Africa 7:37-45.

De Napoli, G.A.
1987   "Inculturation as Communication." in Roest Crollius, A.,
            ed., *Inculturation IX: Effective Inculturation and Ethnic
            Identity*, pp. 69-98. Rome: Pontifical Gregorian University.

Dwane, S.
1988   "Gospel and Culture." *Journal of Black Theology in South
            Africa* 1:18-25.

Echols, J.K.
1984   "White Theology: A Contrast to Black Theology." *Dialog*
            23:27-31.

Ela, J.M.
1986   *Africa Cry.* N.Y.: Orbis.

Fitzgerald, J.P. (Archbishop) & Hurley, D. (Archbishop)
n.d.   *World Bishops Meet: Report on the Rome Synod.* Pretoria:
            SACBC.

Flannery, A., ed.,
1984   *Vatican Council II: The Conciliar and Post Conciliar
            Documents, New Revised Edition.* Grand Rapids: Eerdmans.

Füllenbach, J.
1981   "The Incarnational Aspect of Mission." *Verbum SVD*
            22:325-341.

Fuellenbach, J.
1987   *The Kingdom of God: The heart of Jesus' message for us
            today.* Manila: Divine Word Publications.

Fuellenbach, J.
1988-1989   *Theology of Liberation: Philosophical Theological Background
            and Main Thrust.* Cyclostiled Notes of the Professor, Rome:
            Pontifical Gregorian University.

Geertz, G.
1973   *The Interpretation of Cultures.* N.Y.: Basic Books.

George, F.E.
1987   *Inculturation and Communion: An Essay in the Theology of
            local Church according to the Teaching of Pope John Paul II.*
            Unpublished doctoral dissertation. Rome: Pontifical Urban
            University.

Gifford, P.
1987   "Africa Shall be Saved: An Appraisal of Reinhard Bonnke's
            Pan Africa Crusade." *Journal Of Religion in Africa*
            17:63-92.

Goba, B.
1979   "The Role of the Black Church in the Process of Healing
            Human Brokenness." *Journal of Theology for Southern Africa*
            28:7-13.

Goba, B.
1980   "Doing Theology in South Africa: A Black Christian
            Perspective." *Journal of Theology for Southern Africa*
            31:23-35.

Goba, B.
1982   "The Role of the Urban Church: A Black South African
            Perspective." *Journal of Theology for Southern Africa*
            38:26-33.

Goba, B.
1986a   "A Theological Tribute to Archbishop Tutu." in Tlhagale, B.
            & Mosala, I.J., eds., *Hammering Swords into Ploughshares*,
            pp. 23-30. Basingstoke: Marshall Pickering.

Goba, B.
1986b   "The Black Consciousness Movement: Its impact on Black
            Theology." Mosala, I.J. & Tlhagale, B., eds., *The
            Unquestionable Right to be Free*, pp. 57-69. N.Y.: Orbis.

Gqubule, S.
1974   "What is Black Theology?" *Journal of Theology for Southern
            Africa* 8:16-23.

Grasso, D.
1975   "Evangelizzazione. Senso di un termine." in *Documenta
            Missionalia* 9:21-47. Roma: Editrice Pontificia Università
            Gregoriana.

Greinacher, N. & Muller, A., eds.,
            Evangelization in the World Today: Concilium no.114. N.Y.:
            Seabury.

Green, C.
1986   "Christology and Tyranny: Southern Africa Today: The Kairos
            Debate." *Journal of Theology for Southern Africa* 55:49-55.

Guttierez G.
1973   *A Theology of Liberation*. N.Y.: Orbis.

Haleblian, K.
1983   "The Problem of Contextualisation." *Missiology* 11:91-111.

Häring, B.
1983   *Proclamare la Salvezza e Guarire i Malati*. Lecture notes of
            the professor, Rome.

Hebga, M.
1982   "Sorcellerie et Maladie en Afrique Noire." *Telema*
            32,4:5-48.

Heyns, R., ed.,
1986   *South Africa 1986. Official Yearbook of the Republic of
            South Africa. Twelfth Edition - 1986*. Pretoria: Bureau for
            Information.

Hoeckman, R.
1981   "Christian Mission." *Angelicum* 58,3:312-322.

Hulsen, C.
1976   *Tentative Final ETSA (Evangelisation Today in South Africa)
            Report.* Typed Manuscript. n.p.

Hulsen, C.
1979   *The Churches and Apartheid in South Africa, with Special
            Reference to the Catholic Church.* Cyclostyled, Bound Book.
            n.p.

John Paul II
1986   *Dominum et Vivificantem.* The Lord and Giver of Life.
            Encyclical Issued May 18, 1986. English Translation: *The
            Pope Speaks* 31:199-263.

Jacob, S.
1986   "Kairos: New Trends in Theological Process." in *PCR
            Information (World Council of Churches Programme to Combat
            Racism, Special Issue: Challenge to the Church, The Kairos
            Document and Commentaries.* pp.46-50. Geneva: W.C.C.

Jubber, K.
1982   "Black and White Priests." in Prior, A. ed., *Catholics in
            Apartheid Society,* pp. 124-140. Cape Town: David Philip.

Kairos Doc.
1986   *The Kairos Document: Challenge to the Church.* Braamfontein:
            Skotaville.

Kaufmann, L.
1988   *Pastoral Ecclesiology for Southern Africa.* Hilton:
            Cornerstone.

Kiernan, J.
1976   "The Work of Zion: An Analysis of an African Zionist
            Ritual." *Africa* 46:340-355.

Kiernan, J.
1980   "Zionist Communion." *Journal of Religion in Africa*
            11:124-136.

Kiernan, J.
1981   "Themes and Trends in the Study of Black Religion in
            Southern Africa." *Journal of Religion in Africa*
            12:136-147.

Kunnie, J.
1986   "Christianity, Black Theology and Liberating Faith." in
            Mosala, I.J. & Tlhagale, B., eds., *The Unquestionable Right
            to be Free,* pp.153-167. N.Y.: Orbis.

Lamola, J.
1988   "Towards a Black Church: A Historical Investigation of the
            African Independent Churches as a Model." *Journal of Black
            Theology in South Africa* 2:5-14.

Lavine, T.Z.
1984   *From Socrates to Sartre: The Philosophical Quest.* N.Y.:
            Bantam.

Leatt, J., Kneifel, T. and Nurnberger, K.
1986   *Contending Ideologies in South Africa.* Grand Rapids:
            Eerdmans.

Lederle, H.I.
1986   "The Charismatic Movement - The Ambiguous Challenge."
            Missionalia 14:61-75.

Lopez Gay, J.
1988   *Lo Spirito Santo e La Missione.* Roma: Editrice Pontifica
            Università Gregoriana.

Lobinger, F.
n.d.   *Towards Non-Dominating Leadership: Aims and Methods of the
            Lumko Series.* Lumko: Lumko.

Loewen, J.
1976   "Mission Churches, Independent Churches, and Felt needs in
            Africa." *Missiology* 4:405-425.

Lumko Missiological Institute,
n.d.   *Small Christian Communities.* Delmenville, Transvaal: Lumko.

Lutzbetak, L.
1981   "Signs of Progress in Contextual Methodology." Verbum SVD
            22:39-57.

Maimela, S.S.
1981   "Man in 'White Theology'." *Journal of Theology for
            Southern Africa* 36:27-42.

Maimela, S.S.
1986   "Current Themes and Emphases in Black Theology." in Mosala,
            I.J. & Tlhagale, B., eds., *The Unquestionable Right to be
            Free,* pp. 101-112. N.Y.: Orbis.

Maimela, S.S.
1988   "Theological Dilemmas and Options for the Black Church."
            Journal of Black Theology in South Africa 2:15-25.

Makhathini, D.
1973   "Black Theology I & II." in Becken H-J., ed., *Relevant
            Theology for Africa,* pp. 8-17. Durban: Lutheran Publishing
            House.

Mbali, Z.
1987   *The Churches and Racism.* London: SCM.

Mbiti, J.S.
1971   *New Testament Eschatology in an African Background.* London:
            Oxford University Press.

Mbiti, J.S.
1977   "Christianity and African Culture." *Journal of Theology for
            Southern Africa* 20:26-40.

McCann, D.
1982   *Christian Realism and Liberation Theology: Practical*
            Theologies in Creative Conflict. N.Y.: Orbis.

McElvaney, W. K.
1980   *Good News is bad news is good news...* N.Y.: Orbis.

McGreal, F.
1988   *Missionaries and the Ministry of Healing in the Light of the*
            Experience of Selected Southern African Societies.
            Unpublished MA Dissertation, University of London.

Mcgrath, P.
1974   "Catholic Charismatic Renewal." *Journal of Theology for*
            Southern Africa 7:30-40.

Mermelstein, D. ed.,
1987   *The Anti Apartheid Reader: The Struggle agains White Racist*
            Rule in South Africa. N.Y.: Grove.

Mgojo, K.
1986   "Church and Africanisation." in Tlhagale, B. & Mosala, I.J.,
            eds., *Hammering Swords into Ploughshares,* pp.111-117.
            Basingstoke: Marshall Pickering.

Mofokeng, T.
1986   "The Evolution of the Black Struggle and the Role of Black
            Theology." in Mosala, I.J. & Tlhagale, B., eds., *The*
            Unquestionable Right to be Free, pp. 113-128. N.Y.: Orbis.

Mofokeng, T.
1987   "The Prosperity Message and Black Theology: A Response to
            Allan Anderson." *Missionalia* 15:84-86.

Mogoba, M.S.
1985   "Christianity in an African Context." *Journal of Theology*
            for Southern Africa 52:5-16.

Moltmann, J.
1973   *Theology and Joy.* London: SCM.

Moltmann, J.
1979   "The Liberation of Oppressors." Journal of Theology for
            Southern Africa 26:24-37.

Moore, B., ed.,
1973   *Black Theology: The South African Voice.* London: Hurst.

Morran, E.S. & Schlemmer, L.
1984   *Faith for the Fearful: An investigation into new churches in*
            the greater Durban area. Durban: Center for Applied Social
            Sciences, University of Natal.

Mosala, I.J.
1986   "The Use of the Bible in Black Theology." in Mosala, I.J. &
            Tlhagale, B., eds., *The Unquestionable Right to be Free,*
            pp.175-199. N.Y.: Orbis.

Mosala, I.J.
1989   *Biblical Hermeneutics and Black Theology in South Africa.*
            Grand Rapids: Eerdmans.

Mosala, I.J. & Tlhagale, B., eds.,
1986   *The Unquestionable Right to be Free.* N.Y.: Orbis.

Motlhabi, M.
1974   "Black Theology: A Personal View." in Moore, B., ed., *Black
            Theology: The South African Voice Africa,* pp. 75-80. London:
            Hurst.

Motlhabi, M.
1986a   "The Concept of Morality in African Tradition." in Tlhagale,
            B. & Mosala, I.J., eds., *Hammering Swords into
            Ploughshares,* pp. 85-100. Basingstoke: Marshall Pickering.

Motlhabi, M.
1986b   "The Historical Origins of Black Theology." in Mosala, I.J.
            & Tlhagale, B., eds., *The Unquestionable Right to be Free,*
            pp. 37-56. N.Y.: Orbis.

Motlhabi, M.
1988   *Challenge to Apartheid: Toward a Morally Defensible
            Strategy.* Grand Rapids: Eerdmans.

Muzorewa, G.H.
1985   *The Origin and Development of African Theology.* N.Y.:
            Orbis.

Ndebele, N.
1972   "Black Development." in Biko, B.S., ed., *Black Viewpoint.*
            Durban: SPROCAS.

Ngubane, H.
1977   *Body and Mind in Zulu Medicine.* London: Academic.

Ngubane, J.
1986   "Theological Roots of the African Independent Churches and
            their Challenge to Black Theology." in Mosala, I.J. &
            Tlhagale, B., eds., *The Unquestionable Right to be Free,*
            pp.71-90. N.Y.: Orbis.

Nolan, A.
1986   "Theology in Prophetic Mode" in Tlhagale, B. & Mosala, I.J.,
            eds., *Hammering Swords into Ploughshares,* pp. 131-140.
            Basingstoke: Marshall Pickering.

Nolan, A.
1987   "The Eshatology of the Kairos Document." *Missionalia*
            15,2:61-69.

Nolan, A.
1988   *God in South Africa: The Challenge of the Gospel.* London:
            CIIR.

Nolan, A. & Broderick R.
1987   *Theology of Liberation for Southern Africa.* Hilton:
            Cornerstone.

Nolan, A., Connor, B., & Tiernan, B.
1985   *A Guide to Pastoral Planning.* Springs, South Africa: FEDOSA
            Justice & Peace Committee.

Ntwasa, S.
1973   "The Concept of the Church in Black Theology." in Moore, B.
            ed., *Black Theology: The South African Voice.* pp. 109-118.
            London: Hurst.

O'Reilly, G., ed.,
1983   *Towards Christian Unity.* Pretoria: SACBC.

Oden, T.
1983   *Pastoral Theology: Essentials of Ministry.* San Francisco:
            Harper & Row.

Padilla, C. R.
1978   "The Contextualisation of the Gospel." *Journal of Theology
            for Southern Africa* 24:12-30.

Paul VI
1975   *Evangelii Nuntiandi.* On Evangelization in the Modern World.
            Apostolic Exhortation Issued December 8 1975. English
            Translation, Vatican: Sacred Congregation for the
            Evangelization of Peoples.

Pobee, J.S.
1986   "A Time to Speak and Act in God's Light." in *PCR Information
            (World Council of Churches Programme to Combat Racism)
            Special Issue: Challenge to the Church, The Kairos Document
            and Commentaries*, pp. 37-43. Geneva: W.C.C.

Pretorius, H.
1987   "The New Jerusalem: Eschatological Perspectives in African
            Indigenous Churches." *Missionalia* 15:31-41.

Prior, A. ed.,
1982   *Catholics in Apartheid Society.* Cape Town: David Philip.

Roest Crollius, A.
1978   "What is so New about Inculturation?" *Gregorianum*
            59:721-737.

Roest Crollius, A.
1980   "Inculturation and the Meaning of Culture." *Gregorianum*
            61:253-274.

Roest Crollius, A., ed.,
1983   *Inculturation II: On being Church in a Modern Society.* Rome:
            Pontifical Gregorian University.

Roest Crollius, A., ed.,
1984   *Inculturation V: What is so new about Inculturation?* Rome:
            Pontifical Gregorian University.

Roest Crollius, A., ed.,
1986   *Inculturation VIII: Creative Inculturation and the Unity of
            Faith.* Rome: Pontifical Gregorian University.

Roest Crollius, A., ed.,
1987a   *Inculturation IX: Effective Inculturation and Ethnic Identity.* Rome: Pontifical Gregorian University.

Roest Crollius, A., ed.,
1987b   *Inculturation X: Cultural Change and Liberation in a Christian Perspective.* Rome: Pontifical Gregorian University.

Rounds, J.C.
1982   "Curing what ails them: individual circumstances and religious choice among Zulu-speakers in Durban, South Africa." *Africa* 52:77-89.

SACBC
n.d.1   *The Bishops Speak: Vol. 1 Pastoral Letters 1952-1966.* Pretoria: SACBC.

SACBC
n.d.2   *The Bishops Speak: Vol. 2 Pastoral Letters and Statements 1967-1980.* Pretoria: SACBC.

SACBC
n.d.3   *Catholic Commitment on Social Justice.* Pretoria: SACBC.

SACBC
n.d.4   *Why Some Catholics Join Evangelical Pentecostal Churches.* Pretoria.

SACBC
n.d.5   *World Bishops Meet. A Report on the Rome Synod.* Pretoria.

SACBC
1980   *Interdiocesan Pastoral Consultation, 1980 Report.* Pretoria: SACBC.

SACBC
1984   *Pastoral Planning Working Paper.* Pretoria.

SACBC Theological Advisory Commission.
1985   *The Things that Make for Peace. A Report to the Catholic Bishops and the Church in Southern Africa.* Pretoria: SACBC.

SACBC
1986   *Pastoral Letter of the Southern African Catholic Bishops Conference On Economic Pressure For Justice.* Mariannhill: SACBC.

SACBC
1987   *Community Serving Humanity: Theme Paper for the Pastoral Plan of the Catholic Church in Southern Africa.* Pretoria: SACBC.

SACBC
1989   *Community Serving Humanity: Pastoral Plan of the Catholic Church in Southern Africa.* Pretoria: SACBC.

Scholten, D.
1983   "Church Affiliation in South Africa." Appendixes 2,3 & 4 of
            O'Reilly, G., ed., *Towards Christian Unity: A Guide for
            Catholics*, pp. 236-240. Pretoria: SACBC.

Schreiter, R.J.
1980   "Issues facing Contextual Theologians Today." *Verbum SVD*
            21:267-278.

Schreiter, R.J.
1985   *Constructing Local Theologies.* N.Y. Orbis.

Scott, R.B.Y.
1968   *The Relevance of the Prophets.* N.Y.: MacMillan.

Sebidi, L.
1986   "The Dynamics of the Black Struggle and its implications for
            Black Theology." in Mosala, I.J. & Tlhagale, B., eds., *The
            Unquestionable Right to be Free,* pp. 1-36. N.Y.: Orbis.

Setiloane, G.
1975   "Confessing Christ Today, from one African Perspective: Man
            and Community." *Journal of Theology for Southern Africa*
            12:29-38.

Setiloane, G.
1978   "How the Traditional world view persists in the Christianity
            of the Sotho-Tswana." in Fashole-Luke, E., Gray, R.,
            Hastings, A. & Tasie, G., eds., *Christianity in Independent
            Africa,* pp. 402-412. London: Rex Collings.

Setiloane, G.
1986   "Salvation and the Secular." in Tlhagale, B. & Mosala, I.J.,
            eds., *Hammering Swords into Ploughshares,* pp.73-83.
            Basingstoke: Marshall Pickering.

Shelp, E. & Sutherland, R.,
1985   *The Pastor as Prophet.* N.Y.: Pilgrim Press.

Solle, D.
1987   "'The Moment of Truth'. The Kairos Document from Africa."
            Concilium 192:116-123.

Spiegelberg, H.
1982   *The Phenomenological Movement: A historical introduction,
            3rd ed. (revised).* The Hague: Martinus Nijhoff.

Sundkler, B.
1961   *Bantu Prophets in South Africa, 2nd ed.* London: Oxford
            University Press.

Sundkler,B.
1976   *Zulu Zion and Some Swazi Zionists.* London: Oxford
            University Press.

Thom, G.
1986   "An Opportunity or a Temptation, Southern Africa Today: The
            Kairos Debate." *Journal of Theology for Southern Africa*
            55:46-48.

Tlhagale, B.
1983   "Transracial Communication." *Missionalia* 11:113-123.

Tlhagale, B.
1985   "Culture in an Apartheid Society." *Journal of Theology for Southern Africa* 51:27-36.

Tlhagale, B. & Mosala I.J., eds.,
1986   *Hammering Swords into Ploughshares.* Basingstoke: Marshall Pickering.

Torrance, J.B.
1986   "Listening to its Challenge, Southern Africa Today: The Kairos Debate." *Journal of Theology for Southern Africa* 55:42-45.

Tutu, D.
1971   "God - Black or White?" *Ministry* 1:111-115.

Tutu, D.
1975   "Black Theology/African Theology: 'Soul Mates or Antagonists'." in Willmore, G. & Cone, J., eds., *Black Theology, A Documentary History,*pp. 71-89. N.Y.: Orbis.

Tutu, D.
1977   "God intervening in Human Affairs." *Missionalia* 5:111-117.

Tutu, D.
1978   "Whither African Theology?" in Fashole-Luke, E., Gray, R., Hastings, A. & Tasie, G., eds., *Christianity in Independent Africa,* pp.364-369. London: Rex Collings.

Ukpong, J.
1987   "What is Contextualization." *Neue Zeitschrift für Missionswissenschaft* 43:161-168.

Valentini, D.
1977   "Evangelizzazione." in *Nuovo Dizionario di Teologia* (a cura di G. Barbaglio e S. Dianich), pp.470-487. Alba: Edizione Paoline.

Verkuyl, J.
1978   *Contemporary Missiology: An Introduction.* Grand Rapids: Eerdmans.

Verryn, T.
n.d.   "Throw yourself down: A consideration of the main teaching of Prosperity Cults." in SACBC n.d.4, *Why Some Catholics Join Evangelical Pentecostal Churches,* pp.25-28. Pretoria: SACBC.

Villa-Vicencio, C.
1986   *Between Christ and Caesar: Classic and Contemporary Texts on Church and State.* Grand Rapids: Eerdmans.

Villa-Vicencio, C.
1987   *Theology and Violence.* Braamfontein: Skotaville.

Villa-Vicencio, C.
1988   *Trapped in Apartheid.* N.Y.: Orbis.

Waliggo, J.M., Roest Crollius, A., Nkéramihigo, T., Mutiso-Mbinda, J.
1986   *Inculturation: Its Meaning and Urgency.* Kampala: St.
             Paul-Africa.

Walsh, J.
1982   *Evangelization and Justice: New Insights for Christian
             Ministry.* N.Y.: Orbis.

Welch, J.
1982   *Spiritual Pilgrims.* N.Y.: Paulist Press.

Westermann, C.
1967   *Basic Forms of Prophetic Speech.*, Philadelphia: Westminster
             Press.

West, M.
1974   "People of the Spirit: Charismatic Movements and   African
             Independent Churches." *Journal of Theology for Southern
             Africa* 7:23-29.

Witbooi, B.
1986   "Liminality, Christianity and the Khoikhoi Tribes." in
             Tlhagale, B. & Mosala, I.J., eds., *Hammering Swords into
             Ploughshares,* pp. 101-109. Basingstoke: Marshall Pickering.

Wolanin, A.
1987   *Teologia Sistematica della Missione.* Roma: Pontificia
             Università Gregoriana.

Wonderly, W.L.
1973   "The Incarnation of the Church in the Culture of a People."
             Missiology 1:23-38.

Finito di stampare il 31 gennaio 1991
Tipografia Poliglotta della Pontificia Università Gregoriana
Piazza della Pilotta, 4 – 00187 Roma